Just Keep Going

ALSO BY JEANETTE STOKES

25 Years in the Garden

*Hurricane Season:
Living Through a Broken Heart*

35 Years on the Path

Flying Over Home

Following a Female Line

Jeanette Stokes

JUST KEEP GOING

ADVICE ON WRITING AND LIFE

RCWMS | Durham, NC
2016

Just Keep Going: Advice on Writing and Life
Copyright © 2016 Jeanette Stokes

All rights reserved. No part of this book may be used or reproduced in any manner whatsoever without written permission except in the case of brief quotations embodied in critical articles or reviews. For information, contact RCWMS, 1202 Watts Street, Durham, NC 27701, 919-683-1236, rcwmsnc@aol.com.

Printed in the United States of America.

ISBN 978-0-9960826-5-5
Library of Congress Control Number: 2016938806

First Edition, 2016
10 9 8 7 6 5 4 3 2 1

Copies of the book may be ordered from:
RCMWS
1202 Watts Street
Durham, NC 27701
www.rcwms.org
rcwmsnc@aol.com

In loving memory of Sr. Evelyn Mattern,
who helped me understand that
writing takes a long time.

Contents

Prologue   1

1 When I Was Young   5

2 I Might Be a Writer   11

3 Writing Practice   19

4 Slow Down   35

5 Start Over   45

6 Write a Book   53

7 Writing Program   63

8 Practices for the Long Haul   73

9 Keep Going   91

Appendix   97

Acknowledgments   99

Prologue

I never thought I'd be a writer. I sort of backed into it.

I started out as a talker. I loved being around people, and I'd talk to almost anyone. When I was alone, I talked to my dolls. Talking was easy. Writing was harder. Well, more embarrassing. I was never a perfect speller, which meant the teachers were always putting red marks on my papers to indicate spelling errors. And to make matters worse, the one time I tried to write a long story, a play actually, the piece lacked a plot. That was in elementary school, in the 1950s, in Tulsa, Oklahoma. I gave up any notion of being a writer, because of spelling and lack of a plot, just the way some children give up art when they can't draw a perfect horse by fourth grade. Of course, I still had to write for school, but I never thought of myself as a writer.

After I left high school I got one degree in mathematics, another in theology, and wound up being an ordained Presbyterian minister and a nonprofit director. I thought I'd be a mother, like my mother, but that never worked out. I did keep talking. I have spent my adult years speaking my mind, but I didn't start taking my own writing seriously until I was nearly forty.

It seems a little odd to me now that it took years before I noticed my affinity for the written language. I loved Speech class in elementary school, in which we learned about language and diagrammed sentences that filled the blackboard. I was fascinated by modern poetry and some prose in English class in high school. Understanding the work of e. e. cummings was fun, because it was like solving a puzzle. I was good at math, which was applauded as unusual for a girl; so in college, I gravitated in that direction and left my interest in language behind. My math professors didn't seem to care about spelling.

This book is the third in a series published by RCWMS Press that falls in the general category of life hacking or "how to." *Good Busy: Productivity, Procrastination, and the Endless Pursuit of Balance* by Julia Scatliff O'Grady is about how to survive in our sped-up world. *What Matters Most: Everyday Leadership at Home, at Work, and in the World* by Maura Wolf is a primer on setting priorities and sticking with them.

In *Just Keep Going*, I'll focus on writing most of the time, but much of what I say applies to creativity in general. I've learned that the important thing is to just keep trying things without being too judgmental. Just sit down at the writing table or go into the art space and do something, anything. Thinking too much, being too goal-oriented, sours the process. Just create something now and evaluate it later.

I often say that writing and making things are cheaper than therapy. (I'm also a great fan of therapy.) Expressing my thoughts and feelings through writing, painting, and making things is good for my general health. I've written my way through loss and painted my way through grief on more than one occasion.

And what works for creativity seems to work for life as well. When my friends say they don't know what to do, I often say, "Just keep going." What's next will become apparent as you go along.

I wrote this book as a companion in case you want some company in your writing or in your life. Here, I offer stories, reflections, bits of advice, and tricks I use on myself to keep going.

1 When I Was Young
Spelling

According to my mother, when I was tested in kindergarten, I was one of the "readiest" children to learn to read. But then when first grade came along, I didn't turn out to be one of the star readers.

I was a slow reader. Not slow in learning to read, not slow in comprehension, but I read slowly. As an adult, I actually like reading slowly, but my slowness was a problem in "reading group" in the first grade. Some of the children could read out loud at lightning speed. When I tried to read fast, I just got all tangled up and made up words that weren't there. It wasn't until seminary that I learned most listeners hate to hear anything read fast. When I read aloud slowly, I make fewer mistakes, and it is easier for listeners to understand. But in the first grade, I felt embarrassed every time I was asked to read aloud.

I'm not sure who was more embarrassed: the teachers, my mother, or me. My mother was a perfect speller and, at ninety-four, still works several crossword puzzles every day. (I find crossword puzzles intimidating.) She was probably surprised that I wasn't great at spelling.

Feeling self-conscious stopped me from trying to write for fun when I was young. It stops many of us from trying or from keeping on with a lot of things. In elementary school, I decided I wasn't good at art and took to safer crafts like paint-by-numbers and tile mosaics that left less room for humiliation. But as an adult, I began to look at writing and art from another perspective and came to believe that I didn't have to be perfect at spelling or drawing a horse to write or paint.

Since I liked elementary school and made good grades, there was some puzzlement and discussion about my slow reading and my spelling. My mother and teachers worried most over my spelling, but my slow reading was painfully obvious to me in "Library" class (a designated period for reading books and writing book reports). The library, which doubled as the cafeteria, was lined with bookshelves, tall ones that extended above the height of a first grader. We all shared the books, which led to the bookmark race. I always lost the bookmark race. Let me explain.

We never took the books out of the library. We read them during library period, which meant that several children could read the same book at the same time, so long as they had library period at different times of the day. It was an economical system that greatly reduced the chances of books being lost.

Here's how it worked. I'd select a book to read, and at the end of the library period, I'd mark my place with a colorful paper bookmark with my name on it, thus beginning the bookmark race. During subsequent library periods, I'd read along in my book. Other bookmarks would enter the book after mine, pass me, and leave the book while I was still somewhere in the middle. Even if I was the only child who thought of it as a race, I was painfully aware of losing. I bet you never knew reading was a competitive sport. Winners are rarely conscious of those they leave in the dust.

The school librarian (whom I remember as a tall, thin, dark-headed, severe-looking woman) suggested to my mother that if she got me a typewriter and had me type out my book reports, I might see the words more clearly and notice when they were spelled incorrectly. That was ridiculous. I had no trouble seeing the words. The problem was that I didn't know how to spell some of them. And sometimes I made silly mistakes. I spelled out of the spelling bee in the fourth grade on the word *bed*: "b-e-a-d, bed."

I could memorize spelling words and hang onto them long enough to pass a spelling test, but they didn't always stick. I could spell complicated words such as encyclopedia, because Jiminy Cricket taught me how to sing it on the Mickey Mouse Club: "e-n-c-y-c-l-o-p-e-d-i-a." And I was consistent in my approach. I had a habit of picking a spelling and using it throughout an essay or assignment. For instance, I might decide that the word "they" was spelled "thay." A perfectly logical choice, I'd say. *They* rhymes with *lay, say,* and *day,* at least it did in Oklahoma where I grew up. Why shouldn't it have an A in the middle? I would spell "they" as "thay" multiple times in a paper, and whoever was grading it would circle every last one of them. One red circle and a small note would have sufficed. They didn't have to rub it in.

Sometimes I think I was (and still am) too focused on communicating to care about spelling. Did you know that two hundred years ago people cared a whole lot less about spelling than they do now? Until people such as Noah Webster standardized spelling, many versions of a word were acceptable. It was a conservative and a Calvinist impulse to nail down the "proper" spelling of words. People with good memories for how words are spelled won the fight (and in my experience, many of them became teachers in public school). If you ask me, it's rather undemocratic to insist there's only one correct way to spell a word. Who says a brain that can remember bridge cards that have been played or how every word in the dictionary is spelled are better brains? It's like saying everyone should be at least five and a half feet tall. Then tall people think they are better than short people.

Not being a good speller almost stopped me from ever being a writer. Still, I loved to communicate. I was good at grammar, had an ear for language, and turned out to be a pretty good storyteller. I can often tell something is wrong just because it sounds wrong. "Please pass the catsup to Susan and I," sounds as bad to me as a flat note might to a musician.

I enjoyed learning about grammar as a system, especially from Mr. Kennedy, our energetic speech teacher in elementary school who spent hours and hours standing at an enormous blackboard teaching us how to diagram sentences. Sentence construction made sense to me when I could see how various parts of speech are related. (Mr. Kennedy also taught me to stand on a stage and make myself heard all the way at the other end of the auditorium, which turned out to be useful at high school football games and outdoor weddings.)

I was also fortunate to learn something about how to construct a piece of writing. My high school English teacher, Judy Brazinsky, made us write essays every week and must have spent every waking hour of her life correcting them and giving detailed feedback. Though she taught me to write an expository essay, I still didn't think of myself as a writer. But at least I got a good foundation.

I graduated from high school in Tulsa in 1969 and went off to college in Massachusetts totally unprepared for the social and political upheaval I'd encounter. My parents were Republicans, for God's sake. I hardly believed that what happened in Washington, DC, had any impact on life in the middle of the country.

Once I got to Smith, I took a variety of courses, some in the humanities and some in math and science. It is quite possible that I should have been an English or Religion major, but my papers in those classes always came back covered with red marks because of my spelling. Just like in elementary school.

My freshman year, I took General Literature, an advanced English course. I'm not even sure how I got into the class, but I did fine, except that I found the whole process of writing papers and dealing with spelling to be harrowing enough to quell any desire to proceed further in that department. I took refuge in the Math Department, where they didn't really care about spelling. Later, when I came to think of myself more as a writer, I took some pride in having survived General Literature with a "B."

After college, I moved to Durham, North Carolina, to live with a Smith friend and to be near my Amherst boyfriend, who was a law student at the University of North Carolina. After a year of odd jobs, I applied to graduate schools in mathematics, law, and divinity. I settled on divinity school, because I wanted people to help me make sense of how we could claim that God was good and still have children starving in India. Since I liked being in North Carolina, I decided to go to Duke.

I went all through school, including Smith College and Duke Divinity School, without the benefit of a computer or a spellchecker. It was painful. A favorite professor in seminary once insisted I have another human being read my papers before turning them into him. He found all the mistakes annoying. There was nothing wrong with what I was writing, but it bothered him to have to stop and correct the spelling all the time. So I did that for his classes. I got a human to spellcheck for me.

I've gone on and on about spelling, because it was a huge barrier to my ever thinking of myself as a writer. It is possible that you, too, have had experiences that hinder you when you think about starting to write. Perhaps someone criticized you or made fun of something you wrote. Perhaps you got a bad grade on a paper once. The point is that many of us are frightened of writing or think we're not good enough. I learned that it doesn't have to get in the way forever. We can learn to just keep going.

2 I Might Be a Writer

The first inkling I had that I might be a writer, or have any talent in that area, came when I was in Tulsa for a visit sometime in my young adulthood. While there, I ran into a writer named Elizabeth Thompson, whom I had only known as the mother of a boy who was frequently a classmate of mine. She must have asked me what I was doing, and I must have said I was in seminary or writing a newsletter or something, because I remember she said she had always thought of me as a good writer. That was a surprising comment from someone who hardly knew me. She said she remembered a short paper I wrote (in something like the third grade) that was posted in our classroom for Parents' Night. It was about my father running around in the delivery room the day I was born taking pictures with a camera with no film in it.

The story was true. My father, an ObGyn, was allowed in the delivery room during my birth. He was trying to take pictures, but, to my mother's relief, had forgotten to load the film.

Elizabeth Thompson's bit of encouragement stayed with me for years like a seed buried deep in the ground. It was a commissioning or a calling or a naming that I didn't fully comprehend until much later.

I got further confirmation that I might have "a way with words" while I was in seminary. It came as a surprise to be told I was a good preacher, especially since I served as the coordinator of the Divinity Women's Center during my middle year and was known as one of "those angry feminists." Since most of the students were men, I didn't expect them to respond very well to my words or my presentation style. But they did, or at least the professor and some of the students offered positive feedback. One man in the class, who was blind, gave me one of the highest compliments I have ever received. He said I made him see pictures. It was also a great hint that telling stories and using lots of images is generally a good idea in writing.

I was surprised when one of my sermons was included in an early collection of women's sermons. While Helen Crotwell, then the Associate Minister to the University at Duke, was editing the collection for Fortress Press, she asked the Duke Divinity preaching professor which of his students she should include. He said it should be me. So my first publication in a book was my sermon included in Helen's book, *Women and the Word: Sermons*, which was published in 1978. I felt honored to be included in this pioneering collection of sermons by women.

I Might Be a Writer

I was invited to preach at the Duke University Chapel the summer after I finished seminary in 1977. It was a little overwhelming to preach in public for the first time in a grand sanctuary that looks like it should be a cathedral. I was so nervous I had to hold my feet up off the floor when seated to be sure I wouldn't wet my pants!

AFTER SEMINARY

Just after the Dean handed me my diploma and shook my hand at the Duke Divinity graduation ceremony, I turned to a few friends and said, "They'll be sorry."

As the coordinator of the Duke Divinity Women's Center, I had enjoyed gathering women students, planning courses, and lobbying the administration to increase the number of women on the faculty. Since I wanted to continue that work and didn't know of any jobs available that would let me do so, I set about creating a nonprofit organization that would allow me to keep paying attention to women and religion. At the time, I said my goal was changing the landscape of religion in America. I don't know how successful I have been or how successful the movement of feminism within religious communities has been, but that's what we've been about.

The summer after I graduated from Duke, several colleagues and I founded the Resource Center for Women and Ministry in the South (RCWMS) to be of support to women in and entering professional ministry. I moved to Greensboro, North Carolina, that fall, telling friends that if I was going to run this feminist project, I needed to get out from under the shadow of Duke Divinity School. The real reason was that an old boyfriend lived there, and I was still trying to get back together with him. The romance never revived, but I liked Greensboro, found a charming upstairs apartment in an old house, and designated a desk in one room as the Resource Center. I began collecting names and addresses of people who might be interested in feminism and faith.

While collecting names and developing our first few programs and gatherings, I discovered other events that might interest our constituents—events on women, religion, ministry, and social justice that were taking place in the South and around the country. *South of the Garden*, the RCWMS newsletter, was born of a desire to share information about these events. Since a paper newsletter was the best option in those days, I learned how to create one. The calendar only took up part of the available space, so I started writing short articles about events we offered, feminist books that were being published, the Equal Rights Amendment, and other issues just to fill up the pages.

Since I had a newsletter to produce, I simply started doing it—writing—still not thinking of myself as a writer. It was hard, but when there was a deadline, i.e., when we needed to get a newsletter out, I would force myself to do it. I had always been a talker, so I just made myself talk on paper. In the process, I remembered that I actually like writing and can do it well enough.

Over time I stopped merely reporting and began to speak with a more personal voice, to describe some of my life as it was unfolding, and to reflect on the world around me. That's pretty much what I'm still doing.

COMPUTERS

In the early days of the newsletter, I had to create all the text and paste it down on a big sheet of poster board. I typed the words on an IBM self-correcting Selectric typewriter, and then later if a proofreader found a mistake, I had to type the word or phrase again and paste it over the error. If the changes were substantial, I'd have to type the whole thing all over again. It was a tedious process. So when RCWMS acquired its first computer in 1983, it seemed a godsend.

In the January 1983 issue of *South of the Garden*, I wrote, "A miracle has been wrought by modern science and technology and is due to arrive in my office next week: a word processing computer." Since I knew very few people with their own computers at that point, I went on to explain, "A word processing computer is a computer that will help you with writing and editing but will also compute. They now come in a small size, are called personal computers, and take up as much room as a small TV and typewriter. For good word processing you need several pieces: a central processing unit, a keyboard, a video display screen, a program (software) for word processing, and a printer." The price for all of that was steep, around $5,000.

In college and graduate school, writing a paper and typing a paper had been separate steps. When I first got a computer, I was excited about its editing capability.

Imagine putting the scissors and tape in the drawer with the wrapping paper and forgetting how to "cut and paste." Even if you did not finish a sermon until 2:00 on Sunday morning, it would be all in one piece and typed.

You could even leave the sermon in the computer's memory, pull it out at some future date, make a few changes, and use the same sermon again (in a new setting, of course) without retyping it.

When I put away the scissors and tape, I thought it was forever. In this case forever lasted about thirty years. I got them out again for a good reason, which I'll explain later.

***

A decade later, I was praising email. Yes, the communications method that now clogs up our lives was my new favorite thing in 1994. In *South of the Garden* (Aug. 1994) I noted that Mary Hunt (of WATER: the Women's Alliance for Theology, Ethics, and Ritual, near Washington, DC) got me to start using it more seriously. She had created an email network and sent out a WATER update every Friday. I explained my enthusiasm, "Now I talk with colleagues in other cities regularly via email. I like sending messages and getting quick answers without ever having to address an envelope." I continued, "If you want to know more about this brave new world, I'll be glad to try to help you. You need a computer, a modem, and a phone line to begin. We now have an email address. Please send mail."

***

I continued to work at RCWMS for over a decade, fairly happily. We rarely had enough money, which worried me, but we planned conferences and workshops, gathered feminists of faith, and published newsletters on feminism, theology, and social justice. In early 1990, I fell in love with my first husband, moved to Philadelphia for the year,

I Might Be a Writer

and kept right on running RCWMS by doing office work in Philly and attending our meetings and events in North Carolina.

In May of that year, RCWMS sponsored a conference, "The Art of Feeding the Spirit." At that conference, I began to notice that I was drawn to workshops in which we got to draw, make things, sing, or dance. I learned things about myself through those activities and preferred them to endless hours of verbal input.

For instance, Greensboro artist Adele Wayman led a workshop at "The Art of Feeding the Spirit" in which she showed slides of goddesses and of art made by women. She then laid out paper, fabric, string, and glue and invited us to make something. I made a torn paper picture that reflected something about where I was in my life at that point. In the days following the workshop, I found myself decorating things like postcards and letters. Slowly, I was developing an appreciation for the ways creative expression could be part of a spiritual life, and I was starting to look more carefully at what fed my spirit on a daily basis.

I was also beginning to appreciate a spirituality rooted in daily life. Sunlight in the morning, good food, visits with friends, and long walks—all of these were becoming parts of my spiritual discipline. I was beginning to replace conventional forms of piety with other practices such as walking, painting, and writing.

These practices fed my spirit and helped me to keep going. Other people have a variety of practices that renew and support them, which might include singing, swimming, listening to music, walking in the woods, digging in the garden, knitting, sipping tea, or petting a cat.

3 Writing Practice
1992

I've had my share of successes and gotten my way often enough in my life. Privilege, adequate intelligence, a friendly personality, and perseverance have helped me along. Notable exceptions include small defeats such as being chosen last for the softball team in gym class in elementary school (being a small female could be inconvenient), flunking a volleyball serving test in gym class (the ball hurt my hand when I tried to smack it the way the teacher had instructed), and failing a French exam in college (I didn't spell perfectly in English; it wasn't a whole lot better in French). And then there were the large upsets, including my parents' divorce and my own.

I have rarely felt that God or the universe had it in for me, but there was one particularly bad patch in 1992 when three crushing disappointments piled up on one another. That's when I began to wonder whether I had been singled out to not get things I wanted. I was not chosen for a sabbatical grant that would have given me several months of paid time off from my job. I was not hired as the pastor of a church, the only church I was ever actually interested in pastoring. And my then-husband and I did not get pregnant. No break from the old job, no new job, and no children. I was out of energy for my work at the Resource Center and my marriage was slipping slowly down a rocky hill toward its demise. But in the summer of 1992, all I knew was that I had struck out three times.

If there are angels who watch us and wait for the right moment to swoop in and offer the next bit of inspiration, or guides on the path who wait until we are good and lost to offer the next bit of direction, they arrived right on cue. Help appeared one afternoon at Southern Sisters, Durham's local women's bookstore. Ramona, an older curmudgeonly artist friend, thrust a book in my face and said, "Read this book. This book changed my life." God could not have been more direct if she had placed a burning bush in my path on my morning walk.

I bought the book, Julia Cameron's *The Artist's Way*, took it home, and began working my way through the chapters. One of the practices in the book particularly appealed to me, so following Cameron's instruction, I began to write three pages longhand every morning.

Before long, I returned to the women's bookstore and bought an oversized journal illustrated by Durham artist Sudie Rakusin. I started writing at least three pages longhand every morning and filled up this huge book in less than six weeks. I was writing with a pencil, which turns out not to be the best practice; it wears out your hand too quickly.

Writing Practice

I colored the pictures in the first part of the journal and especially liked the first image of a woman with wings spread wide open. I wrote around the edge of the pictures including, "I want to find my wings and fly." I was forty-one years old. Here's the first page.

> October 7, 1992, 10:00 PM
> I bought this big book at Southern Sisters today for this very big project I am working on. I'm trying to make friends with the creative part of myself again. I've never worked in a book this big before. I use 8.5 x 5.5" books mostly. I think I'll mostly write morning pages in this book, but maybe other things as well. It may bother me that it is so big and my lines may wobble around on the page. I may need some lined paper to lay underneath to keep it all straight. [The handwriting veers off at an angle.] Or maybe I will decide to take off at an angle for a while just to see how it affects my brain. Perhaps I've stayed between the lines too long already. So this is the first page of the Big Blue Book.
>
> My affirmation: I notice & appreciate that I have a gift of expression. I notice & appreciate my gift of expression. I'm very expressive. I express myself lots of ways. I'm learning to love that part of myself and to love the forms the expression takes.
>
> I'm working with monsters. The voices that try to silence my expressive-ness. Perhaps I'll list them on the back of this page tomorrow.

There is a lot I want to tell you about what happened as I went along in this writing practice, but first, more about those three things I didn't get. I'm not saying that these three losses were meant to happen or were even the best for me, but they are what happened: no sabbatical, no new job, and no pregnancy. The result of being denied those things meant that I eventually quit my job and took a much longer, and possibly more fruitful, sabbatical a couple of years later. I had far more time to myself than I would have had if I had become the full-time pastor of a church and tons more time and energy than if I had become a mother at forty-one or forty-two. Don't get me wrong, plenty of women cope with all of that—working full-time and raising children at the same time—but my life opened up and made room for new things, such as writing, in ways that it might not have if I had gotten the things I wanted in 1992. When the marriage fell apart, that made even more room for a certain kind of writing and learning, but I'll get to that part a little later.

MORNING PAGES

So I started writing every morning, a la Julia Cameron: three pages longhand. Whatever came into my head. When nothing came, I wrote down the names of vegetables in alphabetical order, but I was rarely without something to say. I added this new writing practice to my morning routine, which already included a half-hour walk. (Some mornings the routine of getting ready for the day seems to take longer than the day itself.)

I soon fell in love with writing "morning pages" and quickly became addicted. The practice of writing in the morning helped to keep my internal conversation going in a more organized way. Cameron recommends using the time to complain and to write whatever you feel, so that the creative work of the day, which comes later, can proceed with fewer blocks. She also includes other exercises, arranged in a twelve-week program outlined in the book, that can help you deal with negative voices in your head, with a variety of blocks to creativity, and with the fear of success.

As I continued to write morning pages and essays more regularly, I discovered that it was important to develop some practices that supported my writing. Some of these could be thought of as spiritual practices. Many spiritual practices happen on a daily basis; they are things we return to day after day. They open us to the divine in ourselves and in the people and world around us. They create spaces where judgment can be suspended and a person can begin to accept herself. They can be meditation, yoga, washing dishes, or even eating breakfast. Any of these can focus the mind.

BOWL

Back then, most mornings, I sat at my breakfast table, ate yogurt and granola, and wrote in my journal. I still write in my journal most mornings, though I have switched to oatmeal.

I ate breakfast out of the same light blue pottery bowls every morning for about thirty-five years before recently switching to oatmeal. (When I made the switch, I changed bowls as well. I thought the oatmeal looked prettier in dark blue bowls.) The bowls I used for yogurt were part of a set of almost periwinkle bowls and mugs I bought at a kiln opening shortly before I graduated from seminary in

1977. I have other bowls, but I was only happy eating my yogurt out of Sue Anderson's hand-turned bowls. I liked the slope of the sides and the ridges left by the hands that shaped them years ago.

I used the same shaped spoon every day. (Still do.) I like the feel of it in my hand. When I travel, I often miss my bowls and spoons. It's never quite the same eating out of someone else's bowl. Eating breakfast out of a familiar bowl every morning is a practice that soothes me.

Nearly all of life is out of my control. But at least breakfast most mornings is not a surprise. In general I like improvisation. I keep my knees bent, ready for whatever comes. But it's really nice not to have to start making up my life or responding to the unexpected until after breakfast. I just get up, fix "my" breakfast, and write.

But it takes more than a bowl and spoon to make me truly happy while writing. It also takes the right table and chair. I'm short, so tables and chairs are often a problem. My square wooden breakfast table beside a window provides a fine place to write, but the table is a little bit too high for me. Thank goodness it has cross braces underneath that are several inches off the floor. I put a pillow in the chair and my feet on the cross braces, and then I'm comfortable.

For those of you who are taller than 5'1", this struggle with furniture may only be a faint memory from childhood, but it is a constant problem in my life. Not being able to reach one's feet to the floor can cause tightness in the upper back and general crankiness. Having the table fit is as important as the bowl and spoon. Comfort matters. If I'm uncomfortable or if my hand hurts, it is harder to concentrate on writing, and it is already challenging enough to get going and to keep going. I'm all for eliminating barriers that can be easily removed.

BLUE INK

Soon after starting the practice of writing morning pages in a paper journal, I discovered that my hand got tired if I used a conventional ballpoint pen. (I had already made the switch from pencils.) The simple effort it takes to press the pen against the paper for twenty to thirty minutes made my right hand ache. I learned from Natalie Goldberg (*Writing Down the Bones*) that writing would go better if I used a pen that the ink flowed out of with only the slightest pressure on the page. Flair pens, magic markers, roller balls, and fountain pens all met the criteria for ease of writing, but since the first three were disposable and would quickly wind up in the landfill, I set out to learn about fountain pens.

Born in 1951 and starting to school in 1956, I was never taught how to use or maintain a fountain pen. I had used refillable pens for art projects, but the pens belonged to a friend who took care of them if they got clogged up.

I purchased a couple of inexpensive Parker fountain pens, one dark blue on the outside and one burgundy as I recall, and some refill cartridges and began to write with them. It was true. I could go on and on for hours, well, at least for thirty minutes, without hand cramps. But because I was writing every morning, I quickly accumulated a pile of spent cartridges, small translucent tubes that had no further use. That's when I started refilling them myself.

I no longer remember who suggested the refill method I adopted, but I went to the drugstore and bought two or three syringes, cut off the sharp end (to avoid stabbing myself), purchased a bottle of ink, and refilled my pens. I have reused the same plastic cartridges for years, and only keep a few brand new pre-filled ones on hand as backup cartridges for travel. (I've never figured out how to plug up the ones I refill so they don't spill during transport.)

I've had many adventures with these pens. In addition to happily reporting my daily activities, recording the endless stream of thoughts that fill my brain, and writing portions of books with them, I've had a pen explode when I opened it on an airplane, making a mess on my notebook and hands. I've also had ink spew out when inserting the needle into the cartridge and pressing the plunger. A tiny air bubble can form at the opening of the cartridge, and when it bursts, little drops of ink fly everywhere.

These misadventures led me to become a fan of blue water-based washable ink. Once I switched to this less staining ink, I've been happily filling fountain pens and writing with them ever since.

I tried more expensive fountain pens but never found one I liked very well and always returned to the garden variety Parkers. Until my second husband gave me a yellow fountain pen made by Lamy. Lovely to look at and quite comfortable in my hand, it quickly became my pen of choice, and the Parkers were relegated to a desk drawer. Now I have several Lamys, identical except for their outside colors: yellow, spring green, and turquoise.

They give me joy. One morning a few years ago, all the pens were charged and ready to write. That's because the day before, I found them all to be empty and wrote with a back up disposable fountain pen that a friend had given me. I refilled the pens later that day. All those pens standing at the ready gave me a sense of endless possibilities. The next morning, I wrote with the yellow one, with great enthusiasm, for about half an hour.

In addition to using a fountain pen, Natalie Goldberg also suggests cheap spiral notebooks. She is correct in saying that fancy journals are too expensive to encourage the quantity of words one needs to pour onto the page before getting to anything interesting or useful. Mind you, writing is the point, not getting anywhere, but the pretty books seem insulted by page after page of rubbish.

So I bought cheap spiral notebooks and filled them with words. As time went on, I filled cardboard filing boxes with notebooks, almost never looking back at any of them except to pull out a date or detail for a piece I was working on. Somewhere between storage box number two and number three, I grew tired of the way the metal spirals tangled with one another and switched to only slightly more expensive composition books stitched at the spine. These open flat, the most important feature in a journal, and they resist the urge to attach themselves to one another in storage.

These stitched journals also tend to have slightly nicer paper, increasing the pleasure of moving the pen across the page. My favorites are made by ClaireFontaine, but I'm not often in Paris, where they are inexpensive. I also like Moleskin journals and those standard black and white composition books available in office supply stores.

A truly dedicated writer might carry her journal with her, but I am too afraid that I might lose it, or even worse, leave it where some unsuspecting soul might read it. I leave it on a small table next to the breakfast table where I write in the mornings. If I need to capture words on the fly, I write them down on scraps of paper or in a tiny notebook that lives in my pocketbook.

It's important to make yourself as physically comfortable as possible while writing. It is hard enough to keep going; you don't want to let hand cramps or a hard-to-open journal keep you from it.

MANAGE YOURSELF

Even after writing morning pages for a while, I still worried that I didn't have what it takes to be a writer. Then I read Barbara Sher's *Live the Life You Love* in 1996. She says you don't have to change yourself to get what you want, accomplish the things and have the life you want. You just have to figure out how to work with yourself. She says it is important to:

> Pay close attention to what you love, and never listen to anyone who tells you to be practical too early in the game. You don't have to quit your job and mortgage your house, but you do have to turn those dreams over and give them a careful look.[1]

I was relieved to read that "no personality makeovers

---

[1] Barbara Sher, *Live the Life You Love in Ten Easy Step-by-Step Lessons* (New York: Delacorte Press, 1996), 6.

are necessary. You are fine just as you are."[2] No need to "practice self-discipline or self-improvement." But here's the secret. "You will need to find out what motivates you, so you'll treat yourself right."

So all I had to do was learn to work with the person I am. For example, I like to write in the morning, and I like to do it almost every day, at least a little. Other people may prefer to do projects all at once, to write for days and days without stopping except to sleep a little. We are all different. It's really just a management issue—learning how to work with ourselves.

I'm now working on my sixth book using my "little bit at a time" method. It's hard for me to believe. Twenty years ago, I was still trying to figure out how to make a book out of essays I had already written, and I was feeling overwhelmed. I now use the same method for any big project: break it down into small doable pieces. As my office-mate Mary Russell says, "You can't ride a bicycle from here to California, but you can ride from Durham to Burlington, North Carolina, and the next day from Burlington to Greensboro." You just keep going.

When working on a writing project, I try to work on one small section at a time. Not even a whole chapter, just a few paragraphs at a time. When I'm planning a conference or art exhibition, I write down lots of steps (phone calls, an email announcement to design, a reception menu to consider) and focus on them one at a time. Taking on small bits one at a time helps to keep me from feeling so overwhelmed, whether I'm planning a big event or writing a book.

---

[2] Ibid., 7.

WALKING

In addition to writing, I have other practices that support me, walking and making art being the main ones. Writing seems to go better when I go for a daily walk and make art several times a week. I get ideas to write about while I'm walking or painting, and I remember to keep a pencil and piece of paper in my pocket for a sudden inspired thought. If I walk and write and make things, I am usually happier about my other work and about my interactions with people.

Walking has been central to my spiritual practice since I lived next to a long thin park in Greensboro in the late 1970s. I found that walking helped me feel better during the day and to sleep better at night. For nearly twenty years after moving back to Durham, my daily walk followed the gravel path around the nearly square East Campus of Duke University. It took just over half an hour, and I never seemed to tire of admiring the ancient trees that shade the campus. I did it nearly every day. Then a year or so ago, there was a lot of road construction along one side of the campus that included the removal of several large trees. That meant one whole section of the path was noisy, dusty, and more exposed to the sun. So I found myself gravitating to walks in the nearby Duke Gardens. I had to drive to the Gardens, but I got to watch the flowers bloom and the landscape change slowly as the seasons passed. That spring I was amazed at the genius of the gardeners who planted enormous beds so that they were strikingly beautiful all year. When the daffodils and tulips faded, something else would already be coming up to take their place. In May, spikey purple foxgloves and big round purple allium (in the onion family) provided bursts of color. In August, blue-black elephant ears, as tall as teenagers, stretched their long stems and giant leaves across the beds.

I love walking the dirt and gravel paths of the Gardens. Walking on concrete tends to make my knees or legs ache. Once when I was visiting in a big city I almost panicked because I couldn't find any place to walk but streets and sidewalks. When I finally found a small park with a playground and an empty baseball diamond, I walked the bases. I was upset about my pending divorce at the time, so I worked through my feelings as I circumambulated the field, covering the same ground over and over: longing, hope, longing, hopelessness. The baseball diamond provided a container for my feelings.

Writing every day is also a good container for my feelings. It allows me to feel held and heard (by myself if no one else). Walking makes the writing go better. Together, walking and writing make everything else seem do-able.

RESOURCES

In those early years of writing morning pages, I found reading about writing almost as addictive as the writing practice itself. I checked a bunch of books on writing out of the library and then bought copies of the ones I liked. (You'll find more resources in the Appendix in the back of this book.) I became a fan of Anne Lamott, Natalie Goldberg, and Brenda Ueland.

I came to know Anne Lamott's work by reading *Bird*

by Bird (Anchor, 1995), her funny, quirky, inspiring, and just plain useful book on writing. The title comes from a time when her brother was in a panic about a report he had to write on birds. Their father, a writer, told the boy there was nothing to do but take it one bird at a time, bird by bird. Lamott's great advice comes from years of writing and teaching writing. She is, for instance, a big proponent of writing "really shitty first drafts," which she says she writes all the time.

In her collections of essays, Lamott writes about her life, her faith, and her crazy relationships. *Traveling Mercies: Some Thoughts on Faith* (Pantheon, 1999) tracks her spiritual development from a California childhood in a nonreligious home to finding a faith community as an adult. She tells of stumbling into a small church in Marin County that turned out to be a good place for her to recover from drinking and find her place with God.

Natalie Goldberg's *Writing Down the Bones* explores writing as a spiritual practice. It encourages a writer to avoid reporting stuff she has already figured out and to get to first thoughts and authentic feelings in the present moment. Goldberg says, "Go for the jugular. (If something comes up in your writing that is scary or naked, dive right into it. It probably has lots of energy.)"[3] You won't ever have to share the parts of your writing that you don't want to.

Ueland's *If You Want to Write* (Graywolf, 1987) is a wonderful book about the process of writing. In addition to useful suggestions for a writing life, Ueland advocates a daily practice of "moodling." You know what moodling

---

[3] Natalie Goldberg, *Writing Down the Bones* (Boston: Shambhala, 1986), 8.

is. It is doodling without a pencil. It is muddling around. Though it is easier for me to "moodle" on vacation, Ueland helped me realize that I need a lot of unfocused, un-programmed time wherever I am; otherwise there is no place for new ideas to take root. A modern version of this includes putting the cell phone down and turning off the computer.

Ueland also recommends taking a walk that is a little too long. I had never thought of it that way until I read her. She says that if you normally go for a thirty-five-minute walk, you spend all that time doing whatever you usually do: getting your exercise, looking at what you are used to seeing. If you take a walk that is longer, perhaps a little too long, you have a chance to think new thoughts, see things differently, or become aware of something you had not noticed before.

One of the things about writing is that it doesn't seem to work very well to be too goal oriented. It's like making art. If you are too focused on the outcome when making art, the art that gets made is often not very good. An artist needs to be in the moment, paying close attention to the instinct for which color, shape, or tone needs to go right here, right now. Thinking about whether the picture is going to look right usually makes it look all wrong. The same goes for writing. Writing goes better when I have time to get lost in the writing and can just let it flow.

4 Slow Down
1993

Trying to find time in each day to write, walk, and moodle quickly made it obvious how busy I was. Reading *Meditations for Women Who Do Too Much* by Anne Wilson Schaef helped me notice that I was in constant motion and busy all day. So I started trying to be more intentional about slowing down, writing, walking, and moodling and understanding each of these as essential ingredients in my spiritual practice.

A trip to a coastal island, quiet time in my backyard, and making art with friends all helped me take a break from doing, doing, doing, fed my creativity, and gave me energy for writing. Here are a few of the practices that have supported me.

OCRACOKE

I got a good chance to practice slowing down for more than a few hours when I went to Ocracoke Island for two weeks in the summer of 1993.

Ocracoke is not just any island. It is a sixteen-mile-long ribbon of sand off the coast of North Carolina that is accessible only by ferry. Undeveloped Atlantic beaches cover the entire length of the long thin island. The little village shows signs of commercial development, but there are no buildings over five stories and almost no glaring neon signs. Driving off of the two-hour ferry, I felt great relief and a sense of being at least somewhat cut off from city life.

For much of the time on Ocracoke that summer, I sat in a white Adirondack chair on a screened porch and stared at a bush. Not just any bush. A white oleander bush in the front yard of a rented cottage.

I sat. With my notebook lying open on the wide flat arm of the chair, I sat. Because the bush was magical. Because gravity exaggerated the slope of the chair and made it hard to get up. Because I wanted to hear the inside of my head. I sat.

Oh, I walked on the beach every day, played in the surf, and watched the sun set slowly over a picture-perfect harbor. But mostly I sat and stared at that bush.

I wrote some. It mattered little what I wrote. What mattered was sitting and not wanting to be anywhere else.

I remember a feeling I often had in college, that the action was happening somewhere else. Back then, I would ride the bus from my women's college to the men's college nearby, certain that if something was going to happen, it would happen to me there. I was still under the illusion that "it" was "out there" somewhere. It's not. I learn this simple fact over and over in a thousand different ways. "It" is inside.

I find that inner peace all too infrequently. I long for the feeling of being in the right place. I knew the feeling as a small child, wrapped up in a bath towel and my mother's gentle arms, sculpting art out of dough scraps in my grandmother's kitchen, telling stories to the dolls in my room. I remember what it felt like to be at home.

I have that feeling too rarely now. The sense of not wanting or needing to be anywhere else. When the "oughts" and the lists and the need to improve all fall away.

I guess that is why I need a vacation from time to time. To stop, if only for a moment, the impulse to make widgets. To stare at a bush, the ocean, or the sky. To know God in the being rather than in the striving.

That's what I found in a chair, on a porch, by a bush, on an island in the middle of the sea.

SITTING IN THE YARD

I took my watch off while at Ocracoke that summer and I've never managed to put it back on. It's not a problem. There are clocks everywhere: on my phone, on my computer, in my car, and all over my house and office. Somehow removing time from my wrist moved the demands of a schedule just a few inches further away from me. Still, I have to be reminded—over and over again—to go slowly.

One spring morning, more than a dozen years after the summer on Ocracoke, I was sitting under the pecan tree in my backyard listening to the chatter of birds overhead and the squeak of a swing in the park next to my house. I was tired and quite happy to be still, and grateful for a soft breeze. A storm earlier in the week had cleared the air and lowered the temperature. It was a perfect morning.

I sat on a black wrought-iron chair I had bought, along with its twin and a side table, from a friend who moved to a downtown loft some years before. I took the chairs home and plopped them down under the tree, where they remained. None of the other furniture that had lived in the backyard had ever been as comfortable as those wrought iron chairs. The two rockers on the front porch are pretty inviting, but once the metal chairs arrived, I discovered the fine Southern art of sitting in the yard (especially in the spring before the mosquitoes arrive).

I watched a small bird feeder at the back of the garden. I had put it out of commission the previous year after losing a struggle with the squirrels, but having acquired a large bag of seed from a neighbor who moved away, I decided to get the feeder out and try again. The squirrels had not yet attacked it, the birds seemed to enjoy it, and I was happy watching them fly to and fro, eat the seed, and perch on the tall wrought-iron crook that holds the feeder.

It had been a busy spring, and I knew there was no one to blame for the shape of my life but myself. If I take on too many commitments, set my standards too high, answer the phone every time it rings, or answer all the email when it arrives, I am the only one to blame.

So I resolved to begin again, to write in my journal for thirty minutes every morning (instead of checking my email first thing), type three hundred words into the computer, and make art more often, even if it is bad art (art that doesn't please me), because those are the practices that feed my soul. And I promised to sit in my backyard and watch the tall flowers dance in the breeze and the birds toss empty hulls from their feeder.

ART CAMP

I'm happier when I'm making stuff. I've been that way since I was a child. In the summers, my mother would pack me up with an art project and drive me to my grandmother's house, where she'd leave me for a couple of weeks. I loved being in my grandmother's tiny town, Grandview, Texas, population 1,000, so different from the big city of Tulsa, where we lived. When my grandmother and I weren't visiting elderly relatives or buying bushels of peaches or corn, I would sit at her dining room table and color with crayons, weave potholders, create paint-by-number ballerinas, or rub grout around one-inch ceramic squares set into the top of a wooden tray.

Years later, I would knit and crochet my way through college, quilt and make hooked rugs in seminary, and sew curtains for my first apartment in the late 1970s. But then, for a long while after that, I was too busy creating a nonprofit organization to make things.

In my forties, when I read *The Artist's Way* and began writing morning pages, the desire to make things began to stir in me again. About a year later, my friend Jewel invited me over to her house to play with watercolors. She had been collecting paints, brushes, and paper for several years and had finally gotten around to trying them out. She was having fun and wanted me to try it, too. So I went to Jewel's house, splashed some paint onto small sheets of paper, and enjoyed it well enough. That was a Saturday afternoon.

The next Tuesday evening, I had what I can only call, "a watercolor attack." I was home alone, which happened a lot, because my then-husband worked late and traveled frequently for his job. All of a sudden, I wanted watercolor supplies, and I wanted them "RIGHT NOW!" So I got in my car and drove to the nearest craft store to get some. I had no idea what I was doing. I didn't know one brush from the next or the difference between brands of paint, but I didn't care. I bought some supplies, took them home, put water in a jar, and started putting paint on paper. I was in love. That was twenty-two years ago, and the romance is still going strong.

I don't think I still have any of my paintings from that first Tuesday night. It's just as well. I used poor quality paint and inferior paper, but I was having fun.

Eventually, Jewel and I went to a watercolor workshop with an out-of-town expert, which was useful but mildly traumatic. I was so intimidated by the roomful of competent artists that at one point, I fled out the back door of the art room in tears. But I stuck it out for the week and learned how to care for brushes, what constitutes good watercolor paper, and some of the differences among paints.

For instance, I learned that if you paint a big fat stripe of phthalo blue across the paper, you will probably be stuck with the dark teal stripe forever. I ruined a painting of a perfectly nice-looking fish by putting a great big stripe of phthalo blue on top of it. I was trying to paint water. When I asked the teacher how to fix it, he just shook his head. But I've never forgotten that phthalo stains.

I paint patterns and colors on large pieces of paper more often than I try to make a painting look like something. I have painted a few landscapes or scenes from places I have visited, like Santa Fe, New Mexico; but since I forgot to learn to draw, realistic art is challenging for me. I wind up painting squiggles, doodles, and flowers that look a lot like the ones I made as a child.

I used to think that if I painted long enough I'd become more sophisticated and stop painting the same patterns over and over. But eventually I came to understand that those lines and shapes are my visual vocabulary—my very own, like my accent or my brown hair. So I just keep making my marks. And since all I'm ever really trying to do is to delight and entertain myself, I just keep doing what I seem to enjoy.

When I quit my job in 1995 and wanted a place to paint, I rented a small space in a neighborhood building that was once a country grocery store. Built around 1900, it was a thriving business for seventy-five years until it could no longer compete with the superstores like Kroger. The interior of the small building is broken up by low walls, which allow the light and air to move through. When I went back to work for the Resource Center for Women and Ministry in the South a couple of years later, the center moved into the building. We now share the space with a landscape designer and a freelance writer. I've been happily working and painting there for nearly twenty years.

During my self-styled sabbatical, Jewel and I decided to ask our friend Danny if he wanted to make art with us. Danny lived in a big two-story Victorian in Durham. Well, actually, he lived on the second floor. For a number of years, he rented out the first floor; but at some point he stopped that, and the rooms sat empty. When we approached him about making art with us, Danny said, "Sure. Let's do it in the downstairs of my house."

Jewel was unemployed at the time, Danny was trying to figure out what to do after a successful career in retail, and I had lots of free time, so we started making art together once a week and called it Art Camp.

The best part was hanging out with each other. Well, that and never having to clean up. We worked at a huge table, in what had once been the formal dining room, and began by making crazy collages. We piled the table and a sideboard with magazines, paper, glue, tubes of paint, old brushes, and half-finished projects. When those surfaces were full, we started in on the floor. Before long the room was so littered with torn-up magazines, snips of paper, glitter, and bits of string that you had to be careful where you stepped.

Every six months or so, one of us would find a broom and clear a path so we didn't fall down. I cringe when I remember the bathroom sink, which was sparkling white when we began and came to look like a Jackson Pollock painting or the utility sink in a fourth-grade art room.

We were grown ups—in our forties—and we were having the time of our lives. When my first marriage broke up a couple years later, I was really glad to have Art Camp for community and support. Eventually, Jewel got another job, Danny decided to move to Mexico, and I went on painting.

Now my art supplies and my office are in the same physical space, which gives me the illusion that I am always about to make art. The sad truth is that days, even weeks, go by without my so much as picking up a brush. Then I'll remember how much happier I am when I'm making things, and I will get out a big piece of watercolor paper, sketch long ribbons of green, orange, and purple with crayons, and paint swaths of watercolor over them. The paint flees from the waxy lines, colors blend to form new colors, and pools get trapped in unexpected places. I can get totally absorbed just watching a puddle of cadmium red blend with a nearby splotch of lemon yellow and then slowly dry on the paper. After that, I add more layers of paint. Then, I look for pleasing shapes or color combinations to use in the next painting. When the finished pieces pile up, I cut them up to make greeting cards and small books, which I sell so I can buy more paint and paper.

The cycle continues, and I go on painting.

5 Start Over
1995

It's possible that writing, making art, walking, and slowing down finally made me want to stop working. After almost eighteen years of running RCWMS, I was worn out. I was, as we say, burned out. I was tired of marching myself around, checking things off of lists, and accomplishing goals. I once described it this way:

> The work had come to feel boring and demanding, the way pushing a pea across the floor with my nose might be. I was pretty good at pushing the pea, but I was really tired of it. Directing a small, perpetually under-funded nonprofit organization can be wearing. Ask any of the droves of good people in this country who do it. I was not unusual. I was tired, as anyone would have been. And I was surprised.
>
> I had always thought that by inventing my own work I could ensure that I'd love it forever. I thought

creating an organization I adored would save me from burnout. I was wrong. After almost eighteen years at RCWMS, I could no longer muster any enthusiasm. The spark had gone out.

I quit my job and took my own self-styled "sabbatical." You might wonder how a person can leave an organization she founded. RCWMS was a nonprofit tax-exempt corporation with a board of trustees. When I resigned, I left the organization in the hands of the board.

I arranged to leave my job on April 1, 1995. The day before, March 31, I attended a workshop on self-publishing put on by the Alamance County Arts Council. I was interested in making a book out of my *South of the Garden* essays. The workshop gave me some useful tips on the publishing world and information to squirrel away for the coming years.

SABBATICAL

On April 1, 1995, I planned to drive to Blacksburg, Virginia, for my friend Catherine's installation as the Presbyterian campus minister at Virginia Tech. Over breakfast at home that morning, I wrote in my journal:

> The day finally came. The first day of my sabbatical. I feel like I ought to want to say, "Hurrah!" But instead it feels like any other Saturday when I'm getting ready to go out of town and have too many things to do.
>
> I'd like to go someplace pretty and paint for a day, but I don't know where that might be. I'd really like to

> have nothing to do today and just putter in my garden
> and then take a nap.

I was tired, but I was moving on to a new chapter in my working life, and I wanted writing to be a big part of it. I hoped that some rest was also going to be part of it.

The main thing I had learned at the publishing workshop the night before was that the vast majority of people who write don't make any money at it. According to the workshop leader, writing can be one strategy to enhance a business that includes public speaking or leading workshops. He mentioned a woman who wrote children's books that he didn't even think were very good, but whose books sold like hotcakes, because they are about one specific location. Another writer he knew published her material as a spiral bound notebook she sold for $65.00 at workshops she led.

At the time I was still wondering about how to get my work "out there." I didn't have a book yet, but I was hoping to publish my essays and then maybe write another book.

I wasn't completely naïve about publishing. I had learned some things from selling books for RCWMS, such as how to figure out what topics were popular and how to write a publicity blurb. But I didn't know much about getting work published. I had edited a newsletter and filled it with my essays, a few of my pieces had been published in the Independent (a local weekly newspaper), and I had written a couple of book reviews when asked, but I didn't know much about making an effort to get my work published.

People often told me they liked the way I write, but I wasn't sure what they liked. My friend Katherine Fulton, the founding editor of North Carolina's *Independent* weekly newspaper, had often said I was a good writer. My friend B.J. said she liked to hear me explain things. But I didn't know where to start. I didn't want to just point to stuff I had already written as proof that once upon a time I had had something to say. I wanted to write new words for a new day, to say to myself, "Don't just sit there, say something!"

But not right then. On the morning of April 1, 1995, I was out of time. I needed to pack and get on the road to Virginia.

BIG GREEN CHAIR

My self-styled sabbatical began once I returned from Virginia. I decided to take three months "off" before trying to decide what to do next. Even though I wasn't sure what to do with myself each day, it was hard not to fill up my time just being busy. One day I sat down in the big green chair in my living room and said to myself, "I'm going to sit here until I actually feel like doing something." I resisted the impulse to get up and run the vacuum cleaner or balance my checkbook. I sat there for the longest time.

I spent several months doing as little as possible and sitting in that chair a lot. My days were organized around eating, sleeping, walking, journaling, and napping. It is amazing how much time those things can take up if you don't hurry them. I tried to take Brenda Ueland's advice and spent a couple of hours a day *moodling*.

I followed my energy, made some art, and took a few art and movement classes. I visited museums and galleries, rented a studio (in the office building where I still work), and led some retreats and classes on creativity and spirituality. I went to bookstores and wrote down the names of books. Eventually I published a book catalog called *Words & Spirit*. Financial support from my first husband allowed me to move slowly through this period.

I realize that very few people have the luxury of a sabbatical, but a long weekend or part of a vacation can give you a short retreat—unstructured time to rest, walk, muse, read, or make art. Taking a meditation or yoga class can also provide a respite. Periods of rest, unhurried reflection, and wandering about feed my creativity and restore my soul.

LABYRINTH

I made frequent trips to San Francisco in 1996 and 1997, because my first husband had work out there, and I no longer had a regular job. On one of these trips, in January 1997, I dressed warmly and took a cable car from our apartment to Grace Cathedral in order to walk their labyrinth. I had fallen so in love with this form of walking meditation at the cathedral the year before that I had vowed to make a labyrinth.

The labyrinth at Grace is a forty-foot circle containing a winding path that leads from the outer edge to the center. The design came from Chartres Cathedral in France, where it was laid into the floor in the thirteenth century. The labyrinth has no dead ends or tricks, so by following the path, a walker will eventually reach the center. The path is just complicated enough to prevent a walker from knowing how far it is from the beginning to the end. When I walk the path, my mind usually gives up wondering where I am or worrying about whether I'm lost and relaxes into following the path.

At the cathedral, I took off my shoes and stepped onto the purple and gray carpet that bore the labyrinth pattern. Back pews in the cathedral had been removed to make room for the large tapestry. I walked slowly, paying attention to my steps and my thoughts, rounding the curves until I reached the center and its six-petaled rose.

As I stood there, my feet were awash in red light, my mid-section in lavender, and my head in the warm golden light of the sun coming through a stained glass window. I stood very still, soaking in the light as though I were soaking in the love of the sun or the love of God the Creator. Then I sat down for a while and watched the red light move slowly across the center of the labyrinth.

I looked up to see which window was throwing all these beautiful colors onto the labyrinth and was startled to see an image of a printing press. Publishing! It seemed like a sign, like a Western Union telegram from God saying, "Write!" I could have been in that spot at any time of day in any season, but I wound up there on the day when the window with the words "The words will stand forever" and an image of the Gutenberg Press threw a rainbow of light on me.

I nearly burst into tears as I stood there with tongues of fire lapping at my feet. I wanted to protest, "But I can't write. I don't have anything to say. No one will listen to me." But a voice inside insisted, "When God says write, you write. When the creative force in the universe says speak, you speak." I was already writing almost every day, but I didn't have much confidence in any of it.

I said a silent prayer that I might feel as determined about writing and publishing as I felt about making a portable labyrinth.

The labyrinth construction project started in the summer of that year. Friends and I worked on the forty-foot canvas labyrinth for months, and just as we were finishing, my marriage was breaking up. It was hard for me to keep going, but I did, we did. In subsequent years, thousands of people have walked the path we created. And I kept on writing.

6 Write a Book
Or How to Get Going

While I was away from RCWMS, I realized I was recreating much of my previous work but without an organization to support me. I was writing, teaching, and planning workshops, which seems to be the work I am meant to do. In the summer of 1997 when the RCWMS Board suggested I return to my old job, it made sense.

As September 1997 began, I felt like I was arriving at a crossroads. I was about to resume my work after a two-and-a-half-year break. Friends and I were finishing the construction of the canvas labyrinth. And my first marriage was falling apart. I've often wondered about the coincidence of these events. At one point I fussed at God, saying that it was not an even trade—my marriage for a labyrinth and a job.

It wasn't a trade, of course. It was an intersection, a place where my inner and outer journeys met.

Let me explain.

In returning to RCWMS, I was intent on changing the focus of the organization. I was tired of planning large conferences with well-known outside speakers. I was hungry for something quieter and more intimate. I wanted to offer others some of what I was learning about taking care of my own spirit. So RCWMS began to offer small workshops focused on spiritual practices. We developed a program on writing and scheduled labyrinth walks as a form of meditation.

There I was—I had my old job back, and my marriage was ending. I was reeling. Some days I could focus on my work and some days I felt like I might run out in the middle of the road shrieking. Every day, I wrote. When I was in a panic, I wrote. When I was about to burst into tears, I wrote. In the morning and in the evening, I wrote, in my journal with a fountain pen and also in a journal I kept on my computer.

I noticed I was developing two voices. One that was completely unedited. That's the one that came through when I was writing with a pen. The other voice was slightly more aware that someone else might hear it. I let my mind wander and wrote whatever I wanted to in my paper journal but kept a low-key editor working when I was typing.

WHERE TO BEGIN?

In writing workshops, people sometimes say they don't know what to write about. I have not had that problem very often, and in the fall of 1997 the words poured out of me. If you don't know what to write, start with whatever you have been thinking about and see if that leads you somewhere. No need to be lofty, philosophical, or smart. Start with whatever is happening right now: the annoying sound the refrigerator is making or the sound of the cicadas outside. Use your senses. What do you see or smell? Write something that is true or something that is not true or something you remember, like the smell of mimosa blossoms in your grandmother's tree.

Flannery O'Connor once said that anyone who survived childhood has enough material to last the rest of their natural born lives.[4] It's true, and I can also tell you that anyone who survives a divorce (or a disease or the death of a beloved friend or child or partner) has more than enough material for a book.

If you write every day, at least three pages longhand, for a year or so, you will surely hit on something that interests you. I think of it like my ancestors might have approached making a garment. First they spun the thread, then they wove the cloth, and finally they could fashion an article of clothing. But it all began with spinning thread. For me, writing every day is spinning thread.

The first book I published was a collection of essays I had already written. Writing essays got easier after I started writing every day, because every now and then, I actually said something interesting or funny or useful or even inspired, and I noticed it. If it was in my

---

[4] "Anybody who has survived his childhood has enough information about life to last him the rest of his days."—Flannery O'Connor, *Mystery and Manners: Occasional Prose* (New York: Farrar, Straus and Giroux, 1969), 84.

handwritten journal, I transferred that portion to my computer journal. Then I could mess around with it, let it remind me of related ideas or examples, and work it up into a 600- or 800-word essay.

The second book I set out to write was about my separation, divorce, and the first couple of years of recovering from all that. Since I wrote furiously through the days and months of being separated, I had tons of thread to work with. Weaving it all together, editing it down into something interesting, readable, and useful to a reader—that was the hard part.

I had other friends who also journaled their way through a divorce. Carter Shelley, a North Carolina clergy colleague, comes to mind. Years ago, her first husband arrived home from a business trip, announced he had met someone on an airplane, and was leaving her. Carter, stunned and furious, began writing immediately. For a while, she said she was going to work her journals up into a book but never did. So when my marriage broke up in a similarly startling way, I remembered Carter's experience. I vowed to myself to write my way through what was happening, and, if I survived the ordeal, to do something with the writing someday.

It took about four years before I could even look at the material I had started writing in September of 1997. When I was finally willing to work with it, I printed what I had in my computer and put the pages in a big black three-ring notebook. I remember showing the notebook to a seasoned writer and saying, "Look, I have a book!" The wise writer said gently, "I think what you have there are some good notes for a book."

"Oh, OK," I thought. "If I have all this good stuff to start with, this shouldn't take long."

Ah, the blissful naiveté of the beginner! It took me five more years to turn my notes and journals into a manuscript for *Hurricane Season* and two more years to figure out how to publish it. When the book came out in 2008, I couldn't believe the whole process had taken so long. The book is a companion for anyone who might experience a similar loss. I wanted to show how awful it was to feel like I had been dropped on my head, to describe some of the things I did to help myself heal, and to demonstrate that healing is possible, all without being too cheerful about the whole thing.

GENERATING MATERIAL

A slightly different version of the question of where to begin is: How do I know where to begin writing each day? Personally, I leave clues for myself. Some days, that's the only way I know where to start or what to do next.

The other day, I was looking through an under-used sketchbook to find the name of a new Winsor & Newton watercolor paint I wanted to order. I found the name but also found a cactus pattern I had painted the week before. I liked it, and I remember making a mental note to repeat it on good-quality watercolor paper. That mental note got lost, but my sketchbook held the clue.

Clues like that keep me going in my writing as well. I often forget where I was when I stopped writing. I can get lost from one day to the next, which is why I keep a little journal for each book-length writing project. I mark my progress and leave notes about what I think I should do the next time I sit down to write.

I learned this trick from the poet Elizabeth Sewell, who spent much of her later life in Greensboro, North Carolina, where I lived in the 1980s. One evening, some friends invited her for dinner and conversation, during which we got to ask her all sorts of questions about her philosophy and her writing process. I remember she said that she never stopped her writing work for the day without making a note about where she should begin the next time.

There is a plaque on my desk that says, "Discipline is remembering what you want." It is a good reminder that writing is one of the things that I want. I don't have to twist myself into some odd shape or do a whole bunch of calisthenics; I just have to remember to do small parts and pieces of the thing that I want.

I regularly forget what I thought I was doing in my art, in my writing, and in my life. That's the reason I leave myself messages and notes like, "Discipline is remembering what you want." "Just keep going." And "Tomorrow begin on page thirty-eight."

WRITING TIME

Sometime after returning to my RCWMS job in 1997, I noticed that the best way to keep my half-time job to half-time was to only work half a day. But if I started in on it in the morning, sometimes I couldn't get myself to stop until I wore out in the late afternoon. So I began a pattern of staying home in the morning to write and going to the RCWMS office after lunch.

At first it was hard to keep my mornings free for writing. I struggled to keep meetings, medical appointments, and even visits with friends out of my mornings. I learned that if a friend from out of town asked, "Can I meet you at 8:45 or 9:00 for coffee?" I needed to say, "No." I had to stick to my plan, or there was no hope of ever getting anything written.

"Just say no" could be the subtitle of this book. I used to say that someone had to be bleeding, dying, trying to give me lots of money, or be a friend from a thousand miles away to get me to give up a morning. I may strike the friend. As for the bleeding, call 911.

The real problem is that while I have had some success at scheduling times for being creative, I have no luck at all forcing myself into a different schedule. Trying to cram a bit of writing into fifteen minutes slots or switching to afternoon or evening writing times never works very well for me. If I give up a morning and say, "No problem, I'll trade that time for something later in the day," it hardly ever works out. I can't keep a bargain like that with myself, because I can't seem to focus as well in the afternoon. Maybe you can. My point is that if you give away all of your time and energy to work or to other people, you are not going to get very far. It's good to figure out what works for you and to stick with it.

It feels like being mean and greedy to say, "No. I can't do it at that time." No, I can't meet people at 11:45 AM for lunch. To do that, I have to stop everything and get ready at 11:00 AM. It cuts off a whole hour, which often winds up being the whole frigging morning. The real secret is that it takes a good bit of staring into space, doing whatever occurs to me to do for a while, before any real writing and thinking occur. It takes a lot of looking out the window, walking on the beach, pulling weeds in the garden, getting lost in my own thoughts for ideas to form. I can't do it when my brain is taken up with other stuff, which is what happens later in the day.

Now, I can edit (your stuff or mine) on demand, for thirty minutes before or after something else. But I can't write like that or at least I can't write anything new or very interesting. I need to feel at least a little bit of space in front of me or I can't do it.

When my friend Marion was working on a couple of projects at the same time, she was often puzzled about which one to work on. With a busy full-time job, the opportunities to write seemed to come in snatches at all different times of the day. One project was writing some rather playful new essays, and the other project was working with some suggestions her editor had made on another collection of essays. I suggested she could use any fresh creative energy she had to work on the essays, and when she felt a little tired and perhaps less creative, she could edit. For me, writing new stuff takes a fresh, limber mind.

WHAT I DO INSTEAD OF WRITING

Even after I figured out the writing rhythm that worked best for me, I ran into obstacles. For example, one spring morning, I was sitting at the desk in my study getting ready to write, when I noticed a particularly dusty spot beside the desk lamp. I grabbed a rag from the laundry room and dusted the patch. Then I saw another one. Before I knew it, I had hauled the vacuum upstairs, moved stacks of books and piles of papers out into the hall, and given my small study a good cleaning. Pleased with my efforts, I swiped my dust cloth across the window blinds and was horrified by the thick layer of dust it collected. Like a woman possessed, I stuck the fluffy brush attachment onto the end of the vacuum cleaner wand and passed it back and forth until the blinds on all three windows were clean. I wanted to jump back, shout "Ta da!" and wait for the applause.

The only trouble is that I wasn't writing. According to *The War of Art* by Steven Pressfield, all that cleaning was merely resistance. That may be true, but it was such a useful kind of resistance, and my theory of cleaning includes going with the energy when it shows up, because it doesn't come that often. I'm not sure that a clean study makes my writing any better, but it certainly gives me a feeling of relief to have eliminated most of the piles. I no longer spend extra energy glancing at them and worrying about whether there's something in one of them that needs my attention.

I've been joking that I have a new organizing system this year. I say I'm trying to be as inefficient and disorganized as possible. (Cleaning during writing time may qualify.) Moving quickly, doing as many things as possible, and being a whiz-bang at all of it has lost its appeal.

I find that if I move more slowly, schedule fewer hours during the day, and do less, I feel better and am happier. I also notice that by being less "efficient," there's more room for things like a conversation with a friend I bump into.

When I'm less hurried, I'm more likely to take in the color of the sky or the feel of the air around me.

In *A Perfect Mess*, authors Eric Abrahamson and David H. Freedman suggest that for most of us the time it takes to keep perfect order may not, in fact, be worth what it would cost. We should use our time for other activities, like writing and making art. Come to think of it, most of the artists I know spend more time making art than organizing their art spaces. Of course, one has to stop periodically to clean up a little, or else there's no room to do anything. But who says an art room or a writing study needs to be as clean and orderly as an operating room? A certain amount of messiness might even encourage random flashes of creativity. The trick is to discover what works best for you.

7 **Writing Program** at RCWMS

My growth as a writer and the development of the RCWMS writing program advanced together. By the early years of the new century, RCWMS was publishing *25 Years in the Garden*, a collection of my essays; I was working on *Hurricane Season*; and the RCWMS writing program was about to be born.

In 2002, Nancy Peeler Keppel, a friend and a former RCWMS trustee, approached me about whether RCWMS might be interested in creating a program on women and creativity. She offered to make a contribution to support such an effort and suggested we might start with women and writing. Nancy's family, the Peelers, invented and still produce Cheerwine, a cherry-flavored soft drink popular in the South. The company had done well, and Nancy, then in her early seventies, had some money to give away.

(I like to remind people at our writing retreats that we are here in part because of Cheerwine.)

I met Nancy in 1980 when a mutual friend arranged for us to share a room at a national United Church of Christ (UCC) women's meeting. I wasn't UCC, but it promised to be a great feminist gathering, so I signed up. When I met Nancy at the Greensboro airport, I thought she was peculiar. She was fifty, and I was not quite thirty. I wondered who in the world this short, insistent, older woman might be.

Nancy grew up in Salisbury, North Carolina, graduated from Duke, married a doctor, and raised her family in Hickory, North Carolina. In the 1980s, she was active in women's issues in the Southern Conference of the UCC, we served together on the North Carolina Council of Churches Committee for the Equal Rights Amendment, and she was on the Board of the Resource Center for Women and Ministry in the South. After a divorce, she moved to Raleigh to be closer to the center of state politics. She was a tireless worker for justice for women, for LGBTQ people, for the poor, and for the world.

When I told Nancy I thought a writing program was a great idea, I figured she'd give us $500 or $1,000 to get us started with some workshops and possibly a retreat. We were good at doing remarkable things with small amounts of money. Nancy wrote us a check for $1,000 in April of 2002, but then, much to my surprise, her family foundation (the Clifford A. & Lillian C. Peeler Family Foundation) gave us $14,000 in June of that year. That was a whole lot more money than I had anticipated.

Writing Program

Since we had the chance to create a more substantial program than I had first imagined, I enlisted two colleagues to help me invent a writing program. Margie Hattori, a writer and editor who was then on our board, and Mary Jo Cartledgehayes, a minister and writer who had once been our intern and was a great fan of our work, were the perfect partners. Together, we came up with a list of things a writing program could offer. The list included:

- Weeklong writing retreats at the beach
- Workshops, classes, and writing groups in Durham
- An annual essay contest
- Support for writers, including a few grants and some fundraising
- Publishing projects

The first workshop we offered was led by North Carolina writer and editor Peggy Payne, in June 2003, and was called "How to Write More and Better: The Psychology of Creative Writing." The annual RCWMS Essay Contest also began in 2003, with winners announced in early 2004. The first Writing Week at Pelican House (at Trinity Center, an Episcopal conference center on the North Carolina coast) took place in late September 2003, with the next ones in May and October of 2004. With these events, our writing program had begun in earnest.

Nancy Keppel made two requests in addition to asking RCWMS to develop our own programs on writing. She asked me to help her edit a collection of essays by UCC clergywomen and to assist UCC Pastor Mary Evans in producing a CD of gospel music. We did both of those things. The collection of essays we edited, *God Speaks, Women Respond*, was published by United Church Press in 2004. *Mary Evans: Happy With Jesus Alone* was produced by RCWMS and Minnow Media about the same time.

Nancy made things happen in the world by pushing. When she'd call me up and tell me to do something, I'd take a deep breath and usually do it. Though she was not exactly critical, you could count on her to have an idea about how to improve almost anything. The only argument I ever won with her was over the color of the cover of our book. She wanted it to be red and stand out. I wanted it to be blue and pretty. When she gave in, I was stunned, and I took it as a gift and a sign of how much she cared about me.

While we were editing *God Speaks*, Nancy had a recurrence of cancer. Since we talked on the phone regularly, I heard regular updates on her health. Her deep faith in God helped her to weather her cancer treatments with grace and humor. When her doctor suggested that cancer patients who fell in love and ate chocolate got along better, she said she'd get right on it. Though she didn't fall in love (that I know of) in the last year of her life, she ate plenty of chocolate. Nancy was full of zest to the end of her days, never losing her appetite or her love of Duke Basketball. She died in December 2004.

Nancy's contributions to the writing program kept coming even after she was gone. After her death, her family's foundation continued their support. Over a seven-year period, Nancy and the Peeler family foundation gave RCWMS $130,000.

That's how the RCWMS writing program began, and we just kept going.

WRITING WEEKS AT THE BEACH

Shortly after we started the writing program, I began to want more than just a weekend away for writing. I wondered whether anyone would pay to go to the beach with me for a week just to be quiet and write. I took a chance in 2003 and reserved Pelican House, a retreat house on the beach at Trinity Center.

Back in the early 1990s, RCWMS friend and trustee B.J. Fusaro could hardly stop talking about Trinity Center, the new Episcopal conference center on the North Carolina coast. B.J. was active in an Episcopal Church in Wilmington in the 1980s just as the camp and conference center were being developed. Operated by the Episcopal Diocese of Eastern North Carolina, Trinity Center's location on a barrier island just off the coast from Morehead City seemed like an appealing venue.

RCWMS had been holding conferences at Browns Summit, just north of Greensboro, but their aging facilities had grown damp and musty, and we were eager to try a new location. During some of our first gatherings at Trinity, we sat out on an old wooden deck facing the ocean. The deck was attached to a one-story cinderblock building perched at the top of the dunes. As maritime storms ate away at the dunes, the deck had to be removed, and before long, the house was torn down. A modern building with large windows and an ample meeting room now stands atop the dunes.

Trinity Center's staff is friendly and helpful, and the simple, modern facilities, nestled among low-slung live oak trees, are quite comfortable. The beach and the shaded paths on the property are perfect for workshop participants and writers to walk and muse.

At first we signed up for spacious sleeping rooms adjacent to the conference center buildings. Then in 1999 Trinity built Pelican House, a retreat house right on the beach. Run by an Episcopal laywoman, the retreat house was available for individual silent retreats. Every time I walked down the beach and passed the house, I coveted some time in the retreat house—with a group.

When the Pelican House director moved away, Trinity began renting the retreat house to groups for quiet programs. They wanted to continue using the house as a meditative space. This happened at the same time RCWMS was building its writing program. The availability of Pelican House and my desire for longer programs coincided. I had grown weary of driving the three and a half hours to the coast, staying for only two nights, and turning around and driving back to Durham.

That very first week in Pelican House, I stayed in Room Seven and enjoyed a view of the beach below the house and the Atlantic Ocean beyond. I've stayed in the same room every time I've come. We decided that the house would be silent all day every day and that we would gather in the evening to read to one another, practices we have continued ever since. It is a little bit of heaven.

It was such a deliciously restful and remarkably productive week for me that when it was over, I didn't want to leave. I remember bursting into tears in the Pelican House driveway. I had found a home away from home. I scheduled two retreats for 2004, one in May and one in September. A year or so later, I tried one in early January.

Though I wondered whether anyone would want to come to the beach in the middle of winter, they did. Many said they liked beginning the year with time to reflect and to write. Eventually we settled into a schedule of a week in early January, one in May, and one in late September.

Women came and they keep coming. Some women come only once, others more than once a year. Year after year the retreats fill up.

We've had writers of fiction, poetry, children's books, and nonsense, academics turning dissertations into publishable books, women trying to put pen to paper (or fingers to keys) to tell a story they had been afraid to tell before, and professors completing works already promised to a publisher. Over time we have had university professors from Duke, Yale, the UNC system, and elsewhere. We've had exhausted parish ministers who were on sabbatical and women who just wanted to look at the sea. The women often arrive tired, stressed, or grieving from the loss of a loved one. As the week goes on, they unwind, sleep more, and begin to write.

A Zen priest who has been with us twice said she comes to "unravel." That's what I try to do. Just let all the strands of life that have entangled me begin to slip away. I drop down into my own thoughts and imagination. I take time to wander about, walking on the beach or through the carefully preserved maritime forest to the dock on the sound side of the property. As I unravel, I begin to hear the inside of my own head, what I've been thinking or feeling, and I write it down. Sometimes, when I slow down like this, I remember experiences from the past, and I write them down. I usually have a project I'm working on, one of the memoirs I have written in the last few years. But in addition to working on the current project, I try to make time to just write whatever comes to me. Being there for a whole week allows me to sink down into whatever I'm working on. The extended time means I don't have to hurry.

It takes a whole week for the outside world to slip away and for me to arrive at anything that feels like focus or concentration. Although the writing I do the very first day of a week-long retreat might be pretty good, in the course of the week, I am able to sink down into whatever project I'm working on. Sometimes I wander all around in my thinking, in my computer files, or on the Internet looking for things. Sometimes I write long rambling pieces or have a new idea about how to shape a piece of work. However it works out is good. These weeks by the sea get me going; they put gas in my tank. I draw on that energy for weeks afterward. I often find that my energy and focus run low as the weeks go on. By the time another retreat rolls around, I'm ready to be refueled.

I love to sit in the window of Room Seven, look out at the sea, make notes in my journal, sip a cup of tea, and wait for a dolphin to swim by. From this heavenly perch, the world is almost always beautiful. Pelicans pass low across the water, sea gulls squawk, and sometimes a cormorant sits atop the water, spreading its wings to dry.

As I sip my cooling tea, I often feel like the luckiest person in the world. The most amazing part is that being there is part of my job. Being at Trinity Center has been so satisfying to me and to the women who have attended our retreats that we have returned nearly every year ever since we first went there in 2003.

WRITING GROUPS

As the writing program grew, we added more workshops. One of my favorites is an RCWMS-sponsored workshop that local writer and editor Carol Henderson leads each year in March. I met Carol when Sue Versenyi, a poet who came to Pelican House with us, died of cancer and left Carol and me in charge of publishing a book of her poetry. Since Sue had an MFA in poetry, I had assumed she would find a publisher for her wonderful collection of poems but promised that if she didn't, RCWMS would publish them. She didn't find one before she died, so we published *Enough Room* in 2007.

In March of 2009, Carol Henderson led her first workshop for us, "Mining for Gold." I find her particular combination of warmth, humor, inspiration, and pushing to be just the right formula for me, and I tend to write more in her workshops than almost anywhere else.

Some of the RCWMS writing workshops led to ongoing writing groups. I have run at least three such groups over the last fifteen years. The groups go on until participants run out of energy, people move away, or they switch to another group.

It took me a while to figure out that there are many kinds of writing groups. In "critique groups," writers read their work, and others offer comments or suggestions. In "prompts groups," people write together in response to a prompt. Some groups are discussion groups in which people pose questions or ask for help with problems they have run into, while other writing groups are more like support groups.

At some point, I grew weary of writing groups made up of people who weren't writing. Saying you want to write and not writing is like saying you want to eat and not eating anything. Though it may be a bother to fix the food, if you want to eat, eat something, and if you want to write, write something.

Six or seven years ago, I attempted to remedy the non-writing situation. I combined a couple of dwindling groups into a Friday morning group that met at my house and tried a new format: half an hour of "check in" about our lives and our writing, half an hour of actual writing, and then half an hour of reading aloud and discussion. It worked. We were all writing for at least this half hour. The five of us, all women in our fifties or sixties who work in caring professions, have plenty to talk about, but it is so much more satisfying when we actually write and share what we have written.

I'm pretty happy with the group now. I know that on the Friday mornings when the group meets, I'll have at least half an hour of trapped writing time. Being in the company of others who are writing, in a class or in a writing group, often makes me more productive and helps me keep going. Finding a supportive group might help your writing also.

8 Practices for the Long Haul

As I've said, I never planned to be a writer. I became a writer, an editor, and a nonprofit manager without setting out to be any of those things. I had thought I would be a mother, a mathematician, or maybe a politician. Life hardly ever happens the way we imagine, and in my case, I'm glad of that.

Sometimes jobs happen, and as a nonprofit director I had to fill up blank newsletter space, and then divorce happened, and then this newsletter writer published a book of her essays, because "living well (i.e., publishing a book) is the best revenge." And the next thing I knew using metaphors and making my friends laugh turned into the thing I want to do the most and the thing that will probably also torture me for the rest of my life.

Just Keep Going

Some days I wake up thinking, "I'm going to give it up. I'm simply going to stop trying to write." But I don't. It's too seductive.

I've discovered a secret: if I write just a little bit every day, it eventually adds up to being a book. It's amazing. If you walked west from Durham for just one mile every day, in about 2,500 days (that's seven years), you'd be in California. But you'd have to be able to tolerate the going. It's not easy. One young man I met explained that he gave up writing because, as he said, "How would you like to have homework for the rest of your life?"

That is what being a writer feels like. It's worse than the two years I studied Hebrew with a retired seminary professor. I went to the professor's house in the next town once a week for an hour but then suffered for the remaining hours of the week, because I wasn't doing my homework. The homework hung over my head ALL the time. Every time I looked up from my job or my dinner or got home from a nice walk, I'd think, "I've got to do my Hebrew homework." I loved the professor and had to learn the material before I could be ordained as a Presbyterian minister, but it practically ruined two years of my life.

That wasn't torture enough. Shortly after I finished learning an acceptable amount of Hebrew to satisfy the Presbyterians and was ordained as a minister, I stumbled into thinking of myself as a writer. Because I noticed I had been writing. And then, as the young man who gave up writing said, I had homework every day. Permanently. For the rest of my life.

Some days, I resent having homework every morning; but other days, I appreciate the assigned task, because it helps me remember what I want. Writing every day is something I want to do. And I often feel better after I've done it.

One morning during a writing retreat at Pelican House, I accidentally woke up at 4:30 and was writing before 6:30 AM. I felt so virtuous, as though the day was a success before I had even eaten breakfast. All day when I thought, "I should be writing," I could congratulate myself by saying, "You already did that before 6:30 AM."

I will admit that I bounced in and out of bed between five and six o'clock that morning, because I was at the beach, had a window facing the ocean, and kept getting up to see if the sun had turned the horizon pink yet. When it finally did, I started wondering whether I should go out for an early morning walk. Was that the day for my sunrise walk? I often get one when I'm at the beach, usually on the morning I accidentally wake up too early. But my body kept wanting to crawl back in the bed, which I did. But then I read the funny piece by the mommy writer, and my brain clicked on, and I heard, "I didn't plan to be a writer." I opened the computer and wrote much of what you have just read on the last two pages.

I didn't see that sunrise from the beach; I watched it in snatches from the window by my computer. The miracle of a new day was going on just beyond my mist-covered window facing the sea.

And then the second-guessing starts again. Did I make the right choice? Was writing 750 words better than walking by the sea at dawn or better than lying in bed and getting the other two hours of sleep I'm sure I needed? I've long said that creativity is about choices, and I make them every day. So do you. You might consider writing some of them down.

WRITING TAKES A LONG TIME

Once, when I was struggling to keep going and having serious doubts about my writing, I mentioned it to my friend Sr. Evelyn Mattern, and she offered encouragement. When I complained that editing my first book of essays was taking too long, she reassured me that "writing just takes a long time." Knowing that I wasn't doing anything wrong was some comfort, and at least in this instance, my being slow wasn't the problem. Writing just takes as long as it takes.

There are a number of ways to arrange dedicated time for writing. I use the daily writing method. Sr. Evelyn used to take summers off from her work at the North Carolina Council of Churches and use the time to write. She said she simply couldn't get any writing done when she worked full-time as the council's social justice officer.

Her arrangement with the council developed over time. After she had worked there for a few years, and the council was struggling to raise her salary, she suggested they just give her more time off. Eventually she had three months off in the summer. She used this time to be quiet and to write, completing two collections of poetry, *Blessed Are You: The Beatitudes of Our Survival* (1994) and *Why Not Become Fire? Encounters with Women Mystics* (1999). She also created a readers theater piece for the NC Council of Churches, *The Women's Coffeehouse of Spirit: The Chang-*

ing Role of Women in North Carolina Protestant, Catholic, and Jewish Congregations Over the Last Forty Years (2003).

Evelyn was a nun, but not the regular kind. She left her order after Vatican II and joined a new group called Sisters for Christian Community, a non-canonical order, meaning no pope or bishop was in charge of them. She was a tireless worker for justice. I once heard her say, "The price of freedom is constant vigilance."[5] The struggle for justice requires that we pay attention and keep at it. So does writing.

FEELING LIKE IT'S NO GOOD

I discovered that whatever was happening in my own life was often the best source of material for whatever I was writing. Here's an example. After my marriage broke up, I wrote an essay called "Compost" that ended this way:

Weeding creates space and helps to condition the soil. Where the dirt is soft and well worked, weeding is easier. Weeds like to grow in these spots, but it is also easier to pull them out.

> It is similar for the human heart. It is the breaking of a heart that opens it and softens it over time. Well-worked soil grows both weeds and flowers. A soft, open heart can bear both joy and sorrow. Sorrow does not get stuck so easily in a heart that is soft. Pain passes through a heart that is open. Wisdom and joy are able to grow there with ease.

---

[5] Often attributed to Thomas Jefferson, Patrick Henry, Wendell Phillips, and others. See discussion: www.monticello.org/site/jefferson/eternal-vigilance-price-liberty-quotation#footnote2_4muhqxy

Just Keep Going

When I finish writing an essay, a collection of feelings often arise. The first feeling is often: "Whew! That's about done." But not long after that, another feeling creeps in, one that says, "That's about the stupidest thing anyone has ever written." My heart clinches. I freeze. And if, God forbid, I've just read the thing out loud to a group of people, I desperately want a hole to open up in the floor and swallow me so I can disappear.

Finishing the piece about compost was one of those times when I felt unsure about what I had written, so I sent it to my writer friend Mary Jo for some feedback. Here's a bit of our email exchange:

> Mary Jo: "Compost" is a practically perfect piece. You write exquisitely.
>
> JS: Well, that is strong language. I don't get that at all, but thank you very much. I don't see it. I write this stuff and then these eight-foot tall people enter the room all in black and say, "It is crap. It is all crap." When I read your words above, you should hear the chorus in my head, "Why is she saying that? She must be nuts. Who does she think she is kidding?"
>
> Mary Jo: Will you please mail this piece? Just do one last change and put it in an envelope and take it to the post office and then go have a nice cup of tea. Your goal isn't getting into print—that will come—or even collecting rejections. It's simply to put one thing in the mail.
>
> JS: Yes, yes. You are right. That is a great approach. The goal is to put something in the mail. Yes, yes. Of course.

Practices for the Long Haul

It is hard to keep going when the voices in my head are saying, "Your writing is no good. Why are you doing this anyway? No one is ever going to want to read this stuff. You are wasting your time."

I now understand that I am hardly ever able to silence the voices. They live inside of me. There's no way to stop them. But over time, the practice of just keeping on with the writing has proven the voices wrong. Some people do seem to appreciate what I write. And it certainly seems to be good for me to organize my thoughts and experience and write them down. It even allows me to feel that an experience has been examined, considered, integrated into my life. I might even be able to stop picking at it like a peeling sunburn.

The voice that says, "This is boring, this is crap, no one will ever want to read this" is always there. I can't make that one go completely away. So I treat it like a cranky friend and say, "I know," and I just keep going. There is no way to find out if the voice is right or wrong except to finish whatever it is you are working on.

Sometimes I'm able to entertain the various critics in my head by giving them something else to think about, such as how to get someone to paint the garage; but most often, I just have to acknowledge them and say, "I know that's what you think, but for now, I'm just going to keep doing what I'm doing."

The voices tend to be the loudest at the beginning of a project and right near completion, so I've learned to watch out for them at those times and try not to be stopped by them.

It's the same when I'm making art. Sometimes while I'm painting, I'll think, "Oh, this will never work." It happens frequently, especially in the first half of the process. I paint patterns, and sometimes they look ugly to me in the beginning. But if I just keep going, adding more layers, more contrast, some big splashes of color, some tiny little dots, sometimes, not always, but sometimes, the painting will begin to settle down, hang together, and might even please me. If I start with a red, a yellow, and a blue and just keep going, the shapes and patterns and colors will start to work together. It's like a pasta dish: any pasta, any vegetable, any cheese, and some tomato sauce and you almost always get something quite edible.

Painting and writing feel similar to me. In writing, I just need to keep producing the words, even though a lot of them will never be shared with anyone. In painting, a lot of the paper will never become part of anything. Some of the words will get reworked and added into something later on. Some of the paintings will be painted over, and some of them will be used for the cover of a book or a card. But if I don't continue to write every day, there won't be any words to shape into essays. If I don't paint at least sometimes, there won't be any painted paper to make into other things.

I'm beginning to see how this works. I do not have to write brilliant, insightful, scintillating prose every day. I just have to keep writing. Some days I will have good ideas, and some days I'll be as boring as a phone book; but writing is the goal. Just keep going.

WEEDING AND EDITING

I used to hate editing, but over time I came to appreciate it as a crucial part of the writing process. It's the inevitable step that follows generating lots of material.

Writing and editing are different. They may even use different parts of the brain (writing is more like painting or playing around for me, and editing is a bit more like solving a math problem.) But nearly all writing requires editing. (Mine certainly does.) Even the best writers have to have an editor. I once heard Anne Lamott give a reading in a bookstore in Berkeley, California. She reminded the audience that her stuff doesn't come out on the first try the way it winds up on the page of one of her books. Motioning to the back of the room, she said something like, "Just ask my editor."

When I get to the editing stage of my own work, I try to get help as soon as possible. (I've actually come to think of writing as a group project. Out with the image of a writer locked in a room alone for years at a time. In with the image of women sitting around a quilting frame.) I have one editor who seems to like messy manuscripts. So I send her a draft as soon as the English sentences begin to tell a story and I can, with a straight face, actually call it a first draft.

I have another editor who is really good at straightening out sentences and paragraphs that have gotten all tangled up or have become wooden and boring. I like working with her when I get to the stage of fine-tuning the language. When I get completely stuck, I simply say to her, "Do you have any idea here?" She almost always does.

If you say you don't like editing, let me break it to you gently: editing is writing. Let me put it another way.

I have a garden at the back of my yard. Before my current husband dug the whole thing up and made new beds, I had been gardening in the same plot for about twenty years. The garden was well established, if not well kept. The oregano had gotten as big as a doghouse. Sometimes I planted vegetables, but the farmers who sell at the local farmers market do it so much better that I took to buying vegetables and planting herbs and flowers, especially perennials that take care of themselves and come back each year on their own.

In a well-established garden, gardening is mostly about removing things, clearing out, making space so that what is there can breathe and grow. (I prefer a whole lot of plants crammed into a small plot, but eventually some of the little darlings will strangle others if you don't take some of them out.)

While crawling around under the perennials, I remembered that Nancy Goodwin of Montrose Garden in Hillsborough, North Carolina, once said, "Weeding is gardening." I agree. It is only when I'm weeding that I get down close enough to the plants to really look at them and think about what they might need. Editing is similar. When I approach something I have written with fresh eyes and pretend to be the reader instead of the writer, I often notice what's missing or come up with a better example.

There's no way around the fact that weeding is hard work. So is editing. They both require clearing out. Generating words on paper has never been the problem for me. The hard work is editing—making choices, deciding what to leave out.

Practices for the Long Haul

Life is also like that: it's about figuring out what to leave out. Even now, in my sixties, I have more ideas and interests than time. Plus I have a husband, a bunch of friends, and several elders who are over eighty (in-laws, a stepfather, and a ninety-three-year-old mother). If I add walking, making art, working for RCWMS, and even a tiny bit of housework, there simply are not enough hours in a day or a week. So it's a constant challenge to pick and choose among the things I want (or think I ought to want).

The good news is that I've gotten better at editing over time, or perhaps I've just gotten to be more ruthless. When editing other people's work, I warn that I'm not nice. Poor writing makes me want to weep and tear my hair. I prefer editing with a friend, ganging up: two editors to one writer. That way, I have someone to commiserate with. If you complain too much to a writer, she will find it demoralizing.

I subscribe to the three-draft method of editing, which I learned from Stuart Horwitz and his brilliant books, *Blueprint Your Bestseller* and *Book Architecture*. I write everything I can think of in the first draft, and tear the book apart and reshape it around a central point for the second draft. This has brought scissors and tape back into the editing process, tools I thought I had given up when I first started using a computer. Physically cutting up a manuscript and moving the pieces around turns out to be a great way to see what's going on. The third time through a manuscript is for fixing very specific problems. After that, I stop and go looking for a proofreader. Three drafts are usually enough, and besides, I've got other things I want to write about and a life to live.

WRITING ABOUT OTHER PEOPLE

Workshop participants often ask about the problem of writing about people they know. Some people are so distressed at the proposition that it stops their writing completely. We all have stories to tell about important figures in our lives, but we worry over telling tales about family members, revealing long held secrets, or expressing buried feelings about friends or colleagues. Rightfully so. I think we should be concerned about what we say about the people we know (and even some we don't know), but it's hard to write about our lives without mentioning any of the other people in it. And it is boring to only write happy and complimentary things about everyone. Here's the way I've come to understand this topic.

It's important to write it all out even if you don't use it. Describe the person or the events in detail. If you don't, you will leave a big hole in the story. If you decide you can't use it, which has happened to me more than once, at least you will know what it is that you can't say, and you will have a much clearer idea of how to work around it. Your workaround will be more thoughtful and intentional than if you left the whole issue fuzzy.

Be prepared! Even if you are thoughtful and careful in your selections, some people will be pissed off. Of course you are uneasy when writing about people you know, but you can only write your version of the truth as you have experienced it. It is your life, and it is okay to write about it. That said, it's not a good idea to work out your lifetime grievances in print. Published work is mostly for the enlightenment, education, or entertainment of others. You are the only person who can weigh the costs and benefits of speaking publicly about your friends and relatives. One option may be to create disguises or composites, but this only works sometimes. I know of a man who wrote a whole book that was a thinly disguised tale of the town where he lived. Too thinly, as it turns out, since many people figured out who was who and many local residents stopped speaking to him.

One safeguard is to ask people to look over what you have written about them. I do this when I genuinely want someone's input, but sometimes I just do it as a courtesy. The first time I published a book that mentioned a lot of people I knew, I shared pertinent passages with nearly everyone who was mentioned in the book. I've eased up on that practice somewhat since I've written and published more. I now have an internal barometer that will say, "You need to check that out with so-and-so." This has been especially helpful when the people I'm describing have been able to fill in details that I didn't know or had forgotten, or when they had a slightly different memory. But I never promise to take all of their advice or suggestions, even when I am happy to have their input.

In other cases I have not shown people what I've written about them. Nor have I asked their permission. This includes some of my relatives, some people I have not seen in forty years, and people whose political views I do not share. Caution would be advised here, as this is a dangerous approach. I know a writer who received hostile responses from family members after publishing a book that was, in places, unflattering to the family and their history. As I recall, they told her ahead of time that they would be upset. She told me that she was not sorry she published the book, but the whole experience was very hard on her. Broken relationships can be the result of telling your version of the truth.

Publishing a book that includes a lot of material about one person can be a special case, especially if the person is likely to see the work. I actually got a signed release from the person who stood to be most upset by *Hurricane Season*, the book I wrote about my divorce. I sent a manuscript to my first husband for him to review and a form for him to sign. This made me incredibly nervous. My advisors and attorney said I had to do it. Please note, I am not an attorney, and you should not take this as reliable legal advice. If you write about people you know, and you say anything they might not like, you would be well advised to consult a lawyer. Truth is a defense against libel, but it will not protect you from being sued, which is expensive, time consuming, and emotionally draining.

Perhaps there should be a disclaimer printed on writers saying, "If you are my friend, you run the risk of showing up in what I write. You don't actually have much control over that. And if I outlive you, you may never even know." Since it isn't feasible to brand all of us, it may be important to remind friends that you do write about people you know and that they should be clear when they are telling you something they don't want repeated. Writers are wise to use a measure of commonsense and respect for other humans. Some stories are simply not mine to tell.

When writing about other people, remember that the landscape is full of internal quicksand and external alligators. Get support from other writers. Tread carefully in writing about people you know, because there is no guarantee that your subjects will thank you.

ADVICE WHEN STUCK

One writer friend complained that she had a cold and wasn't getting any writing done. When she asked if I had any wisdom on the matter, I said:

> 1. Get over the cold.
> 2. Your job takes nearly all of your attention, even though it is part time. As an introvert, you are probably so depleted by the extroverted nature of your job that takes everything out of you. As I recall, you like to be rested and to have lots of space and time around you in order to write.
> 3. Imagine the job is the same as if you were an English teacher. English teachers say they simply cannot write during the school year. (Art teachers say about the same thing about doing art.)
> 4. Look at the times on your calendar that do not have travel or the job in them (I mean weeks or months). Put the writing in those times.
> 5. Schedule some writing retreats for yourself and don't give the time away because you get asked to do something for someone else.

Actually, writing is the only cure for not writing.

I haven't mentioned writer's block, because I have no experience with it and consequently no stories or advice. I think that writing is the only cure for not writing. For that matter, writing is the cure for most anything that ails us in the writing process except writing. Writing is the cure. If

Just Keep Going

I feel jealous or despondent or uninspired, writing is what there is to do.[6] Well, meditating is also a good approach, but I recommend it as a predecessor to the writing. I often use writing like meditating. If I will write out what is in my brain, I can see it, and then sometimes the difficult feelings will shift into something else.

It used to bother me that some of the best writers I know don't write. Sometimes I would try to figure out things I could do to get them to write. But then I remembered I once heard an artist friend say that he wasn't the best artist he knew, but he was an artist who would do the work. Talent is only part of the formula. My friend had enough talent to paint, show his work, and sell paintings, so he kept on being an artist. I don't think of myself as a good writer; I have just come to know myself as a writer who will write, a writer who will keep going. Consequently, some of my work gets out there into the world while the brilliant thoughts and beautiful words of other people may stay hidden.

I finally had to give up worrying about people I think are good writers but who don't write. They stand in a long line of people I don't need to fix or change. It's silly to think I could even if I tried. My job is to keep my desire to change other people in check, stay on my own path, and get back to writing.

---

[6] For a discussion of jealousy, see Bonnie Friedman, "Envy, the Writer's Disease," *Writing Past Dark: Envy, Fear, Distraction, and Other Dilemmas in the Writer's Life* (New York: HarperPerennial, 1993), 1-8.

HOW TO WRITE A BOOK

If you want to write a book, here's some advice that I've gleaned from a variety of sources:

- Turn off the TV, the radio, and the Internet. Stop going to movies. Stop going out to lunch with your friends. Stay home (or wherever you write) four times as long as you think you can stand it.
- Write thirty minutes longhand first thing each morning. Just do it.
- Write every single day. Don't miss one. Try to write at least 300 words, even if it is garbage.
- Carry a piece of paper and a pencil with you at all times.
- Do the full twelve weeks of *The Artist's Way*.
- Take a class or workshop on the kind of writing you want to do.
- Join or start a writing group or create a virtual writing group. I need companions on the writing journey, and you may need them also.
- Be prepared to give your life over to this. Saying, "I think I'll write a memoir," is sort of like saying, "Oh, I think I'll build a house." In order to do it, you have to do it, and you wind up thinking about it all the time.
- Read books about writing, but be careful not to use up all your writing time reading about writing. Some of us would rather read about writing than actually write.

9 Keep Going

One day in 2009, I wrote for almost two hours in the morning, an hour or more in the afternoon, and then I edited for two hours that evening. The next day, I said something about this to my friend Liz, who was once a journalist. I told her I don't see how reporters do it—write all day. She said, "They don't," and added that two hours of writing per day is about all most humans could manage. I was surprised. I had been feeling like a total wimp, a fraud, because I could only manage an hour, or two tops, on the mornings I set aside for writing.

A few years ago, I heard author Jane Yolen read at a local bookstore. She has published over 170 books, many of them wonderful historical fiction for young people. In the Q&A, I asked a question I like to ask writers, "How do you get your work done? How are your days structured?" Yolen said that she writes for eight to ten hours a day. Maybe I heard her wrong. Maybe she said she works for eight to ten hours a day, spending some hours on correspondence or finances. Whatever she does, it works for her, and she has all those books to show for it. I have felt like a fake ever since.

In *Bird by Bird*, Anne Lamott says that if you write 300 words a day, you will have a book in a year. That's even with time out for birthdays, Christmas, and going to the doctor. Three hundred words is about one double-spaced page. I thought she meant, "Any dummy can write 300 words a day." I took her at her word and started writing 300 words a day in my computer. That was about twenty years ago. Those files sometimes turned into books, such as my writing from 1997 and 1998, which became *Hurricane Season*. The daily writing became other things, such as articles for the RCWMS newsletter. But it was never more than an hour or two.

As I've said, I have rearranged my life so that I can write in the mornings, and I am very strict about that schedule. No appointments. No work for RCWMS. Not too much email. (OK, I cheat on that a lot!) Nothing, except sometimes exercise and the Friday morning writing group once a month. That's all.

I do write, though I feel like I'm really slow. I keep at it, and somehow I keep finishing manuscripts and publishing books. A little bit at a time. A little bit every day.

Writing is all about making the time to do it. A few years ago, a writer friend and I came up with a new writing practice. We call it T.W.T. (Trapped Writing Time). We do it virtually, when I can be at my computer and she at hers. We pick a starting time, show up at our desks, and email each other, saying "OK, go!" Then we write for forty-five minutes, or until we can't stand it any more, and then e-mail, "How are you doing?" Writing in tandem like that helps me keep to the task.

We like to say that T.W.T. is a B.I.T.C.H., which stands for "Butt In The Chair, Honey." We have learned that if you don't sit down to write, writing never happens.

JUST KEEP GOING

I was about twenty when I attended my first Zen Buddhist *sesshin* (meditation retreat). I remember only a few things about the weekend retreat held in the Field House at Smith College. One is the crack in the floor, which I observed for hours on end. Another is that when it was over, I said to myself, "I've done that now. Won't have to do that again." The most striking thing I remember, however, is an instruction given by the Japanese *roshi* (teacher) who led the weekend. He said that when we listened to his teachings, we did not need to struggle to remember what he said. He promised that anything of real use to us would find its way inside of us and take root. He was right. The one thing I remember from his talk is that I didn't have to struggle to remember what he said.

Writing isn't so much about struggling as it is about staying with the process. Charlotte, North Carolina writer Judy Goldman put it well in an interview in a North Carolina Writers Network newsletter (2004):

> Perseverance is what it's all about. It's not really about talent. There are a lot of people with a lot of talent,

> but not a lot of people with perseverance. It's all about staying with it, no matter which part of the process you're engaged in, whether it's the writing of the book—so many people begin a novel and don't finish it…. Then when you get to the publishing process, it's so easy to give up…. It's all about perseverance and staying with it.

As a child I discovered that if I stuck with a club or a camp long enough, eventually they would let me be in charge. As a young adult, I learned that the people who get PhDs are the ones who don't give up. Later on, writers insisted that writing is really slow work and encouraged me not to become discouraged. Judy Goldman assured me of that. Don't give up. Keep going.

It took from 1995 to 2002 to finish and publish *25 Years in the Garden*, the first book of my essays, and that was after most of the essays had already been written. With *Hurricane Season*, it took five years to get over the separation and divorce enough to even look at my journals, and then four years to write the book, get other people to read it, cut out a hundred pages, and rewrite it more than once.

When writing, I frequently hear a voice in my head saying, "This is junk. Why are you still working on this?" I reply, "Maybe so, but this is what I am doing, and I am going to keep going." I try to finish a project and then let people I respect help me decide if it is worth publishing. I'm telling you this in case you write and think your writing is garbage. Read it out loud. Get into a writing group. Share it with someone else. How will anyone ever know what your life is like if you don't tell them? If you need

Keep Going

help with the prose, there are people around who are more than willing to assist you.

And as for whether you are writing the right thing or not, it's not really up to you or to me. Just keep going. And pray. You might use Thomas Merton's prayer,

> My Lord God, I have no idea where I am going...and the fact that I think I am following Your will does not mean that I am actually doing so. But I believe that the desire to please You does in fact please You.

Finally, it is not the goal but the journey that is important. It is not the finished piece but the writing of the piece that changes me. Writing a book, looking for a lost quote, and repairing a house are all part of the journey. If we seek our own deep wisdom, trust a community of friends, and rely on the presence of God (Buddha, Tara, Shiva, or the Great Unknown), then we may discover again and again that the journey is home.

It's like the roshi was saying: don't struggle. Just listen and you will hear and remember whatever is really important. Life does not have to be such a struggle. Writing doesn't have to be quite so much of a struggle. Just keep writing. Just keep going. There is no perfect way to do it. There is no road ahead. We make the road as we go.

Appendix
Books on Writing

Cameron, Julia. *The Artist's Way: A Spiritual Path to Higher Creativity*. New York: Jeremy P. Tarcher/Putnam, 1992.

Friedman, Bonnie. *Writing Past Dark: Envy, Fear, Distraction, and Other Dilemmas in the Writer's Life*. New York: HarperPerennial, 1993.

Goldberg, Natalie. *Writing Down the Bones*. Boston: Shambhala, 1986.

Horwitz, Stuart. *Blueprint Your Bestseller: Organize and Revise Any Manuscript with the Book Architecture Method*. New York: TarcherPerigee, 2013.

———. *Book Architecture: How to Plot and Outline without Using a Formula*. Providence, RI: Book Architecture, 2015.

———. *Finish Your Book in Three Drafts: How to Write a Book, Revise a Book, and Complete a Book While You Still Love It*. Providence, RI: Book Architecture, 2016.

Lamott, Anne. *Bird by Bird*. New York: Anchor, 1995.

Pressfield, Steven. *The War of Art: Break through the Blocks and Win Your Inner Creative Battles*. New York: Grand Central Publishing, 2002.

Sellers, Heather. *Chapter after Chapter: Discover the Dedication and Focus You Need to Write the Book of Your Dreams*. Cincinnati: Writers Digest Books, 2005.

———. *Page after Page: Discover the Confidence & Passion You Need to Start Writing & Keep Writing (No Matter What!)* Cincinnati: Writers Digest Books, 2007.

Sher, Barbara. *Live the Life You Love in Ten Easy Step-by-Step Lessons*. New York: Delacorte Press, 1996.

Ueland, Brenda. *If You Want to Write*. Minneapolis: Graywolf, 1987.

Welty, Eudora. *One Writer's Beginnings*. Cambridge: Harvard University Press, 1984.

Acknowledgments

This book mentions many of the people to whom I am grateful, people who noticed or encouraged my natural tendency to communicate. Though I never thought of myself as a writer when I was young, several kind souls cheered me on. Over the years, many people have, knowingly or unknowingly, helped me to become a stubborn, persistent, and (much to my surprise) productive writer. They have helped to make my writing better. I am especially grateful to the people listed here.

Mr. Kennedy taught speech at Eliot Elementary School in Tulsa and gave me a love of sentences.

Elizabeth Thompson, the mother of a classmate, noticed that my writing was entertaining.

My father didn't type or spell perfectly, and thereby offered me a genetic excuse for many of my mistakes.

My mother helped me express myself, sometimes by letting me pace up and down in her bedroom, saying what I was thinking as she captured my words on her typewriter. It helped me learn to think well on my feet. She never told me to stop talking, until I got to high school and started recounting the convoluted details of teenage romances among people she didn't know. That's where she drew the line and asked me to give it a rest.

Katherine Fulton offered me my first experience with "word processing" and helped me cobble together pieces of writing for North Carolina's *Independent* in the early days of the newspaper.

A group of six linguists at Georgetown University developed the first spell-check system for IBM and made my life a whole lot easier.

Sr. Evelyn Mattern reminded me that writing takes a long time.

Nancy Peeler Keppel was generous with her love, support, and doggedness. In particular, I am grateful for her vision of an RCWMS program on spirituality and the arts, especially the art and practice of writing. And for her financial gifts that supported the program for a decade. I hope that she is pleased with what we have spun out of her gold.

The Board of Trustees of the Resource Center for Women and Ministry in the South has offered years of enthusiastic support and direction for the RCWMS writing program.

RCWMS board member and dear friend Marcy Litle seems to have retired from Duke just so she can give an afternoon a week of her time to editing our publications.

Acknowledgments

I don't know what we would have done without you, Marcy.

I am lucky to be surrounded by talented young writers who inspire me—Meghan, Rebecca, Erin, Jenny, lizzie, and Emma.

I appreciate all the people who have been part of the RCWMS writing program. Thank you for trusting us with your teaching, learning, sharing, and growing. People who have come to Pelican House writing weeks have created warm and supportive containers for sustained writing time.

Various incarnations of the Friday morning writing group have provided regular check-ins that are, for me, like mile markers on a long journey.

Peggy Payne offered invaluable guidance as I was shaping the manuscript of this book.

Liz, Carolyn, and Emily, my secret grammar council, willingly answer even the most bizarre question about commas, semicolons, and the ever evolving rules of footnoting even if they are on their way to lead a funeral, give a lecture in an English class, or visit family on the West Coast.

Though Kaudie McLean meticulously checked the text with her characteristic grace and care, I have probably managed to sneak in a few mistakes.

My friends have either stopped calling me in the morning or apologize when they do. If I weren't such an extrovert, I'd be disciplined enough to never answer the phone until lunchtime, but I don't always remember that writing time is what I want. So, thanks to those who help me with that.

Dwight, my dear husband, never complains about my insistence on this writing schedule and never makes fun of the fact that it takes me a whole morning to gather my focus and eke out three hundred words. NOTE: This book is published as part of the celebration of the 40th anniversary of the founding of RCWMS. We officially launched in August 1977. We are celebrating for a full year leading up to and beyond August 2017.

Some of the pieces in this book are based on or borrowed from essays first published in *South of the Garden*, the newsletter of the Resource Center for Women and Ministry in the South.